D0269920

.... cat in South London.

Room to Listen, Room to Talk

A Beginner's Guide to Analysis, Therapy and Counselling

Tony Lake and Fran Acheson

Bedford Square Press in association with BBC Radio 4

Published by
BEDFORD SQUARE PRESS of the
National Council for Voluntary Organisations
26 Bedford Square, London WC1B 3HU

First published 1988
© Tony Lake and Fran Acheson, 1988
Reprinted 1989

Typeset by The Word Shop, Rossendale, Lancashire
Printed and bound in England by Billings and Sons Ltd, Worcester

British Library Cataloguing in Publication Data
Lake, Tony
  Room to Listen, Room to Talk
  1. Psychotherapy
  I. Title II. Acheson, Fran III. Series
  616.89'14

ISBN 0–7199–1227–X

Contents

For C, imagined and real . . .
. . . and for V.L.

Introduction

Just looking

If you know next to nothing about counselling, psychotherapy, and analysis except that you've heard of them, this is the place to start.

There are other places you could start, of course. There is already a vast literature on these subjects. Nearly all of it is for counsellors, psychotherapists, and analysts. There are tomes which deal with theory and technique, text books for people studying the skills, the art, and the science of therapy, reviews of research, accounts by people who have been clients or patients, histories and biographies, books which promote ideas and books which de-bunk the promoters. We have listed a selection of them in our bibliography.

So far as we know, however, there are very few jargon-free books written just for clients – and there are even fewer for people who are not yet clients, not even sure they want to be clients, and who are wondering what all the fuss is about.

So what we have tried to do is write a beginner's guide, a book which spells out simply and concisely what counselling, psychotherapy, and analysis do, and what they are for. It is not a consumer's guide, telling you which is the best buy, or awarding five stars to this variety, four to this one, and one for effort to the rest. We have not assumed that you want to buy anything yet, merely that you are intrigued.

Except . . . there is a little more to it than this. For a start, we are both enthusiasts. We are firmly of the opinion that what goes on in counselling, psychotherapy and analysis is generally good for the client. We think that many more people could benefit from it.

Hard to be objective

We make no apology for this, because it is difficult in any case to be completely objective on this subject. Therapy – meaning counselling, psychotherapy, and analysis – is an organised business from which a lot of people are earning money, increasing their own status, and gaining access to people who can easily become dependent upon them. It would be foolish to deny that the practitioners therefore have a vested interest in bringing about a situation where more and more people think that therapy is valuable. Consumers of therapy also have an interest in propagating the idea that it is a good thing – they have almost certainly made a considerable investment of time and money in their particular form of therapy, and are, on the whole, more likely to defend this by being in favour of therapy than against it.

At the same time it is obvious that if we want our questions answered these are the very people we must ask, the people we must quote. We cannot expect them to be completely impartial.

Furthermore, therapy itself – particularly psychotherapy and analysis, but also increasingly counselling – is one of those subjects which is wrapped in mystery. It has its own language or jargon, its own theories, and its own brand of logic. From its inception, external critics have been told that they are unlikely to understand it and will be ill-equipped to make judgements about it unless they have tried it. This is reasonable enough, but it is not the whole story. When the critics try it to see if it works, they are likely to be told that it will only work for them if they suspend their critical faculties and enter into it with a positive commitment in its favour. So you either have to stay outside to criticise – in which case you are told that you do not know what you are talking about – or give up your criticism and become a client.

It also has to be said that the therapies generally are based on a body of ideas which is still controversial in many quarters. Despite the numbers involved, the whole idea that therapy is something which can help people is still rejected by quite a large group of the population, and many who do not reject it outright believe that it is relevant only to a minority whom they see as especially disturbed or mentally ill in some way. Also, certain of the ideas of a good many therapists are rejected by a good many other therapists.

Not surprisingly under these circumstances, people who are interested in therapy tend to be either all for it, or completely against it. We have tried not to go too far either way, however, but to search for a middle road – to show you not just the advantages but also the risks of therapy.

How to use the book

Otherwise the book speaks for itself, but it might be helpful to explain how it is organised. It falls into four parts. The first part looks at the recent explosion of what we call the 'therapy movement', and tries to account for it, explaining broadly what therapy is and where it fits into the health business, going on to look in more detail at the uses of therapy in general. The second part explains the differences between counselling, psychotherapy and analysis, and the third one looks at the processes which are involved – how they work, what we have to contribute to it, and what can go wrong. Finally we consider the choices that are available to you – the different varieties of the therapy and how you can find a therapist, we consider what all therapy has in common, and we take a look at the future of the therapy movement. We also list some addresses you might find useful.

Acknowledgements

A great many people helped us with this book – therapists, clients, ex-clients – not only by giving their time and sharing their ideas, but also by letting us record interviews with them often on very sensitive subjects. We cannot mention them all by name, but we owe them an unrepayable debt of gratitude.

In particular we would like to record special thanks to Katherine Vaughan and Vicky Duffy, and to thank the following therapists who spent time talking to us about their ways of working:

Derek Blows, Ruth Barnett, Jenny Biancardi, Christopher Bollas, David Brazier, Faith Broadbent, Patrick Casement, Prue Conradi, Peter Cook, Neil Crawford, Jill Curtis, Deryck Dyne, Fay Fransella, Penny Greenwood, Dorothy Hamilton, Robin Hobbes, Robert Hobson, Jafar Kareem, Lionel Kreeger, Lionel Monteith, Haya Oakley, Anton Obholzer, Jonathan Pope, Manny Sher, Chris Thorman, Brian Thorne.

We would also like you to consider writing to us c/o the publishers if you have any comments, suggestions, or criticisms – or simply wish to share any feelings you may have about the book.

Tony Lake
Fran Acheson
June 1988

'I didn't see any need for therapy at the start. It was Julie who insisted we should both go. She went for counselling first, because she was unhappy with our marriage, and then started to insist that either I should go with her or find somebody to go to myself. It was either that or she was leaving. I was quite happy with the marriage, but I didn't want to end up with a divorce for no reason so I went along.

'The fact is, once we started the counselling, I began to realise that I had been unhappy for a long time, but simply didn't want to admit it to myself. You don't always recognise it when things are going wrong. You blame the other person, or put it down to stress at work and feeling tired, or just muddle through and say to yourself, that's Julie – the kind of person she is, never very happy, always worrying about something going wrong. All the time, though, it was just as much me as her.

'I was furious with Julie when she pushed me into going. Now I think it's the best thing that ever happened.'
(*Peter, a client*)

PART I
WHAT IS THERAPY?

1 The therapy movement

Phone-in

The studio is a cramped little room in the basement with a hexagonal table in the middle. Six microphones on long stems sprout upwards at orderly intervals like metal mushrooms, and through the window that covers one wall you can see a technician seated at his console and the producer standing next to him. Out of sight around the corner sits the man who answers the phone. He is already busy, talking to one of today's callers, scribbling a note, and trying to attract the producer's attention all at the same time. It is two o'clock on an ordinary weekday afternoon.

'And that's the sports news,' says the announcer. He moves slightly closer to the microphone and shifts his voice down a tone to make it sound more confidential. 'After the break,' he says, 'it will be your chance to talk to our counsellor about any emotional, marital, or sexual problems which are bothering you. The number to call, right now, is . . .' He gives the number.

The counsellor settles into the seat next to him, adjusting his headphones and watching the green video screen next to the clock, alert for the first clues about the person he will talk to soon, whom he will never meet face to face, but who is almost certainly desperate for help. The adverts begin, and details of the first caller take shape letter by letter on the screen: 'Sue, 26, problems with boyfriend.'

Every day this scene, or something very like it, is being duplicated in dozens of other commercial radio stations up and down the country. Sometimes the calls are slow to come in. Sometimes they seem to be falling over themselves to get down the wires, fighting for a place on those green screens. There are hundreds of counselling phone-in programmes each week, and each programme receives ten or more calls for each of the six or seven which are answered on the air. It adds up to hundreds of thousands of calls per year – all from different people who need somebody to talk to, somebody to listen.

In the studio the red light comes on above the control room window. The caller is connected. 'Hello,' says the counsellor, 'Where would you like to start?'

Counselling centre

We are in Paddington, London. A row of massive early Victorian houses with unkempt garden walls looks down on a busy street, a stone's throw away from a street market. An empty drinks can rattles along the pavement in the cold, damp wind. Cars line the edges of the road on both sides, and swish recklessly past each other in the middle. You look at your piece of paper, and then check the numbers written in peeling paint on the stone pillars at the ends of long, steep paths. One house looks neater – signs that it is more cared for than the others, an absence of the draped wires and entry phones that indicate multiple occupancy. This must be the one. The Counselling Centre.

Up the steps and in, carpet softening the sound of your footsteps. There is a reception desk to your right, and stairs ahead of you. You say your name to a smiling, relaxed woman, and soon you are on your way upstairs to a comfortable room where you are greeted by another kind, smiling face. You still feel nervous, uncertain what will be asked of you, wondering if you have done the right thing in coming here. The counsellor closes the door, settles you into a chair, and as she sits down herself she says those same words: 'Hello. Where would you like to start?'

In different parts of the country a similar scene to this one is also being repeated many hundreds of times every day, in modern flats, small cottages, cosy semis, offices and consulting rooms. People who need to talk are meeting people who are trained to listen and help.

Ways of helping

Something important is happening. We are at a moment in history when counselling and psychotherapy, and – indirectly – psychoanalysis, are for the first time becoming a significant mass activity, touching the lives of millions of people. These three ways of helping people, almost infinite in their variety, yet connected together by history, purpose, and practice can be called collectively the 'therapy movement'. Broadly stated, their objective is to enable people to get more from life, to be happier or more fulfilled by becoming psychologically or emotionally fitter.

Only a small proportion of the people involved meet on radio phone-ins. Most of them meet face to face. They will almost certainly be alone in the room together for about an hour, and there will be no interruptions from outside. The two of them sit side by side or face to face, or maybe one of them sits and listens at the head of a couch whilst one lies down on it and talks. One of them, the client, will be troubled, perhaps tearful, maybe angry or nervous, and will be doing most of the talking. The other, the therapist, will be a professional helper, and spend most of the time listening. At times there will be long silences, much longer than you would expect in ordinary conversations or in an interview.

More than a million

Nobody knows for certain how many people each year seek this kind of help, or how many provide it. The British Association for Counselling (BAC) currently has three and a half thousand individual members, each of them a supporter of the counselling movement, but not all of them qualified or full-time counsellors. About 350 organisations are affiliated to BAC – including counselling centres, colleges which hold courses in counselling, and industrial or commercial companies which train some of their managers in counselling skills. A full-time counsellor will probably hold about twenty sessions per week, so if there are only fifteen hundred of them – less than 50% of the membership of BAC – this already adds up to well over a million sessions per year.

Yet the BAC itself represents only part of the therapy movement, perhaps about half. Many counsellors have their own separate associations, linking them with people who share the same body of ideas and who use the same technical approach. The movement also includes many psychotherapists and behaviour therapists who do not belong to the BAC. Then there are people who specialise in marital or family therapy, working with couples or parents and their children together, and therapists who concentrate entirely on group work with people who are not related to one another.

There are also the analysts, probably five hundred or so, members for the most part of analytical societies which provide psychoanalysis within the health services and for private clients. Most of them are to be found in London, running busy practices, training the next generation of analysts, writing and publishing learned papers. They and their founders were the originators of the therapy movement, though a significant part of the movement has been built by people who see themselves as rejecting many of the ideas and methods of 'mainstream' analysis.

Still growing

The therapy movement is big already, and it is still growing. Introductory courses on the use of counselling skills, lasting less than 30 hours in total and run by local colleges of adult education or by the many hundreds of management training organisations are so numerous today that the BAC has given up counting them. Professional training courses, through which people become counsellors in the fullest sense of the word last rather longer. There are currently some 130 of these offering up to three years' training, each adding between ten and twenty newly qualified men and women to the professional ranks annually. Soon there will be more courses. Universities, colleges of higher education, and polytechnics have recognised the huge demand for places and are taking steps to meet it.

The same kind of expansion is happening in psychotherapy. Jill Curtis took over the chair of the clinical service of the British Association of Psychotherapists (BAP), three years ago. At that time there were about eight referrals a week, she says. On the day we spoke to her there were 2,036 people in therapy with members of BAP, and the association receives between 50 and 60 applications per week, mostly self-referrals, although it is not their policy to ask who sent them, only how they heard of BAP. Many of them, incidentally, first learned of the association through LBC, one of London's commercial radio stations. BAP plays a prominent part in the training of psychotherapists, which is also expanding nationally in the hands of many organisations. When we asked the BAC about psychotherapy training, they told us that there are now about 30 nationally recognised five-year courses for this.

Could it help you?

It all means that many more people today are turning for assistance to this relatively new breed of professional, and that the way things are going, if you haven't already done this yourself, then you or somebody close to you soon will do. Our aim, therefore, in writing this book is to give you a better idea in broad terms and simple language of what therapy is, on the assumption that you want to know mainly for personal reasons.

Perhaps you or a member of your family or a friend is contemplating asking for help, or needs help and does not know where to turn. Maybe you or somebody close to you needs help but has not yet recognised this need. Or you may have just started therapy and are wondering what it will be like.

Either way we want to make it easier for you to answer for yourself the question: is this the kind of help that I need or could make use of, or which would be useful to somebody else I know personally?

So – where would you like to start?

Asking questions

We can only begin with questions.

Some of them are about therapy in general. What is it? The word clearly has connections with the idea of healing and with medicine, but what kind of healing is involved, and what is healed? Whereabouts does therapy fit into the whole field of medicine and health? What is the connection between therapy and having problems?

Who is therapy for? It is widely believed that therapy is only suitable for people who have 'real' problems, in the sense that either they have come up against a terrible emergency, or because they are basically the kinds of people who cannot cope with the ordinary stresses of everyday life. Is this true? Who are the people who seek help? Are they people like yourself, members of your family, your friends and colleagues? Or are they very different from you? Why do they seek help – with what kinds of problems and under what circumstances?

What, more specifically, are the three main types of therapy for – counselling, psychotherapy, and analysis? How do they differ from more traditional ways of helping people? What are the particular strengths of counselling, say, or of psychotherapy or analysis, compared with the other two therapies? Are they much the same kind of thing or do they deal with different areas of experience, different problems? How long do they take?

Then there are questions about the methods used in therapy. How does it work? What is the procedure or the process which makes it work? What techniques are used? What does it do to help you solve problems, or to become more like the person you would really like to be? What are the risks you take and the difficulties you are likely to experience? What does it feel like to be in therapy?

We also need to ask questions about the different kinds of counselling, psychotherapy, and psychoanalysis. Each of these three therapies is practised in a wide variety of ways, and we need to explore why this is so, and what the main ways are. It will also be useful to look at some of the theories on which the different varieties are based.

2 Place of therapy

Is it medicine?

We are all familiar with physiotherapy, which is concerned
with helping people reassert control over their body after an
illness or an accident. Most of us have probably also heard of
occupational therapy, which helps people to start their minds
working again after a major illness. You may also have come
across hydrotherapy, which flourished a generation or so ago
and is now less fashionable as a mass treatment, and
electro-convulsive therapy – electric shock treatment – which
is widely used in psychiatric hospitals. In medicine generally,
therapy means the treatment of disease, and is concerned with
all aspects of recovery from illness.

The word 'therapy' comes originally from a Greek word
which means 'servant', one who waits upon somebody else.
Over the centuries it has acquired this additional meaning,
connecting it first with the idea of healing and then with the
idea of medicine.

So when we use the word 'therapy' to refer to counselling,
psychotherapy, and analysis, what are we saying? The obvious
implication is that they are a form of medicine, that is to say,
kinds of treatment for people who are ill. At the same time
nobody would claim that the people who go for counselling,
psychotherapy, or analysis are going there primarily in order
to get treatment for physical disease. The logical conclusion is
that these therapies are to do in some way with mental health.

Before we go any further, therefore, we need to be clear
about the connection between the idea of health – particularly
mental health – and the therapies we are talking about. What
is the place of these therapies in the health world generally?
There is an obvious danger in making wrong assumptions
about it.

Danger of confusion

For one thing, if therapy is mainly concerned with treating mental illness, there will be many people who feel that counselling should not be included in the list. Take marriage guidance counselling, for example. Asking for help to sort out a marriage is clearly not something which indicates that you are mentally ill. And what about career counselling? The people who go to talk to somebody about their next moves in promotion, or about what to do to find a new job after a redundancy are not going because they are mentally ill and looking for a cure.

This applies equally to the other two therapies. Those people who are receiving psychotherapy, or who undertake psychoanalysis may deny vigorously that they are there for this reason. So will their therapists – indeed, there are many general therapists and analysts who will be very chary of taking on clients with a history of, for example, chronic schizophrenia, major drug abuse, or even in some cases, attempted suicide.

The place of all three therapies in the whole business of health care needs to be very clearly defined, not just to avoid this kind of confusion, but also because we cannot hope to understand the usefulness of therapy and why so many people are now turning to it unless we know whom it is intended to help.

Positive health

To place the therapy movement in context, we have to recognise that over the last few decades, a great many people have begun to change their ideas about what health is. This change has been slow and subtle, and is still working its way through the world of medicine and the population at large.

The old idea was that health meant the absence of illness – in other words, that if you do not have illness of some sort then you are healthy. This has been called the negative view of health.

The new idea is much more positive. After all, you may have no actual illness as such, but this does not necessarily mean that you are fit and well in every sense of these words. You may not actually be ill right now, for example, but your recent past history may show that you are prone to get ill – there is a difference between being healthy and being between illnesses. Also, you may not be fit. Perhaps you are over-weight, or

constantly tired, and unable to enjoy life. The new idea of
health is that it means feeling good all over, fit and well, full of
life, not necessarily happy all the time, but being able to enjoy
the good things you have without being set back on your heels
whenever something bad comes along.

New standards

We can see this change in attitude all around us today. It
shows in the way almost every high street now has a health
club or a health food shop. It shows in the upsurge of interest in
alternative medicine, and in the campaign against food
additives. In the medical world itself there seems to be a new
emphasis on prevention, too, particularly obvious in the
campaigns against cigarette smoking, and to alert people to
safer sex because of the threat from AIDS.

When we begin to think of health as general well-being,
rather than the absence of illness, we are doing something else,
too. We are adopting a different standard in our expectations,
accepting that we can and perhaps should get more out of life
than a disease-free existence. We are beginning to say that
everybody deserves a measure of joy, where once we said that
everybody deserves freedom from illness. Of course, it would be
wrong to exaggerate the extent of this change in attitude. It
probably applies only to a minority still, but there are
certainly signs of change.

Mental health

Nevertheless, most of our ideas about mental health have
changed even less. For a whole variety of reasons we are much
more ignorant about mental illness – what it is, whom it
affects, what causes it, and so on – than we are about physical
illness. Mental illness means illness of the mind. A large part
of the problem is that we do not really know what we mean by
the mind.

A century ago this was far less of a problem. In those days
scientists accepted without question that each person consisted
of three fundamental parts – body, mind and soul. Mainstream
medicine dealt with the body, psychiatry with the mind, and
the soul was the province of the priest. They were confident
that one day the physical part of a person which they called the
mind would be discovered, perhaps somewhere inside the
brain.

The problem is that they were wrong. There is no separate

organ inside us which carries out the single function of the mind. What we call the mind is a mixture of things – some of them to do with the way parts of the brain work, some to do with the way that nerves all over our body work, and some to do with the way that hormones are produced and distributed throughout the body. This means that the old way of thinking about people has had to be abandoned. The mind is not something which exists separately from the body, and it is not a special and identifiable part of the body. Rather it is a set of functions carried out by many different parts, some of which have many other duties besides.

Psychiatry

Yet in abandoning the old idea that the mind exists separately, we have so far failed to replace it with a new one which is fully acceptable to everybody. Psychiatry, the treatment of mental illness, has therefore tended to merge into physical medicine. It takes place in hospitals, either specialist ones, or in departments of psychiatry in general hospitals. In this country you have to be a fully qualified doctor of medicine before you can become a psychiatrist, so all the basic training is in physical medicine. It uses drugs which switch off parts of the person's behaviour while he or she is nursed back to a more acceptable state of health. Psychiatry also uses electric shock treatment almost as standard practice for people who are suffering from severe depression.

Very little of this is 'mental' medicine – in the sense of being a mental activity which involves the patient intellectually in his or her treatment. It is something the doctor does to the patient, and in no way depends on the patient's ability to understand what is being done. It concentrates on the brain and the body of the patient in much the same way that treatment of a renal patient is concerned with his or her kidneys, or the treatment of a back patient with his or her spine. The patient is treated and watched and nursed. The causes of the illness are regarded as physical causes – an excess of certain chemicals in the brain, for example. It is rare for a patient in hospital to be encouraged to question the causes of the illness – just to accept the treatment of its symptoms and to take over the medication for himself or herself as soon as possible.

However, this kind of physical intervention is not an appropriate way of helping all the people who feel very depressed, whose lives are made a misery by constant anxiety, whose feelings threaten to get out of control, but who are not seen as ill enough for hospital. Psychiatry tends to be used only for very serious cases – people who actually hurt themselves, who clearly cannot live without being a threat to themselves or others. Below this cut-off point there is a grey area where the general practitioner responds in the main by prescribing lowish doses of tranquillisers and anti-depressants, and keeps an eye on the situation. But if you need help with emotional problems, and do not want to go into hospital or start taking the pills, there is very little that the official medical services can actually do for you.

Where therapy fits in

From this perspective we can now see much more clearly where therapy – meaning counselling, psychotherapy and analysis – fits into the picture. First, it is beginning increasingly to be used to help people from the 'grey area', the people who a decade ago would simply have accepted a long period of dependency on tranquillizers and anti-depressants. They are ordinary men and women who are deeply hurt and unhappy, who have problems particularly where their relationships are concerned, but for whom the psychiatric hospital would be an absurd over-reaction.

A great many of these people are finding their own way into therapy, either going to a counsellor in the hope that this will enable them to tackle a specific problem, or finding a psychotherapist for themselves, because, for example, they have read about this or heard about it on radio or television. Most do not see their family doctor first, although a minority are being referred by their general practitioner and see their therapist at a hospital. There is also a small group of clients who have experienced life as a patient in a psychiatric ward and who have found their way into therapy by themselves out of disillusionment with psychiatry.

Nearly all the therapy that is available is to be found in the private sector, and it is the client who does the finding – you do not need a letter from your general practitioner before you can go to see a therapist.

Secondly, more and more people are beginning to think positively about physical fitness, and as part of this they are also beginning to see very clearly that how they feel in themselves is an important part of the battle for health. They want to be fit, but are recognising that it is extraordinarily difficult to get fit or stay fit if deep down they do not feel good about themselves. As a result they are looking in increasing numbers for ways of tackling the unhappiness. They tend to refer to this as 'emotional' rather than 'mental' health, or talk about spiritual health. But it amounts to the same thing: the connection between our bodies and how we feel about ourselves is a fact of life, and we cannot significantly improve health in one area without tackling the others. They are turning to therapy in the search for positive health.

In the old days people expected to be disappointed with life, and accepted this – living with unhappy marriages, depressing relationships, dull and boring jobs, poverty, general lack of fulfilment. Unable to change it, they made it into a virtue. Today there is much more questioning of the need for this.

Self-help

So a new idea of mental health is emerging, confused and tentative in some respects, and lagging a little way behind our ideas on physical health, but nevertheless growing in influence. It is that mental health today means being able to use all your functions – physical, mental, intellectual, social, emotional – whatever they are, to the fullest extent. People are systems of resources, and full health means being able to use these resources in such a way that we have choices in life, that we know our own value, and can increase this value not just for ourselves, but for those around us and the wider community we live in.

However, people are assuredly not turning en masse to psychiatry for this kind of health. Psychiatry is still seen as being mainly about madness, to do with curing illness. It is still a branch of physical medicine, too, as we have seen. The three therapies on our list are very different from this.

They belong to a different tradition of health – in some ways a much older tradition than that of orthodox, scientific western medicine. They start from the point of view that much of what is wrong has been learned, and can be unlearned. Because they stem from this philosophy, the therapies are concerned with self-education, and with self-management. They enable you to do something for yourself to improve the quality of your own life. At the same time they recognise that it is almost impossible for you to do this entirely by yourself and that professional help of the right kind can make all the difference.

Indeed, history has, in a sense, come full circle, for this kind of therapy is much more in keeping with the original Greek word than modern medicine is. The therapist who is a counsellor, psychotherapist, or analyst is in attendance to help you like a good servant, there for you, not there to take over and do things to you. The therapist is a guide or a mentor, a facilitator, not an expert authority who does things to your body or your mind, intervening in your life, but a new partner with whom you work, a special kind of companion who helps you find your own way forward. Nevertheless there is still enough of the old idea of mental health around for many people to be afraid of therapy. This shows in some of the misunderstandings about it which are commonplace, even today.

It can't happen here!

Many Europeans seem to have a great fear of turning into Americans. One of the things you are very likely to be told if you raise the question of therapy in conversation is that the way things are going, we shall all soon be like them, dashing off to phone our analysts when the slightest little thing goes wrong in our lives. Perhaps this should be called the Woody Allen syndrome – he more than any other film maker has popularised this view of the Americans. The most jingoistic sufferers of the syndrome, however, declare stoutly that 'we are not like that'.

Behind the little joke lies a big fear. We are supposed to be self-sufficient, proud of our toughness. We have a fear of softness. When we have problems we hide them or deal with them ourselves, without making a fuss. So when we think about therapy, there is for many of us a need to make myths about it.

Myths

For example, there is the myth that tough people do not need therapy, or any other help with problems. Therapy is for soft people who cannot cope with the ordinary vicissitudes of life. What's more, if you go into therapy you become soft, and turn into a navel-gazing introvert, endlessly analysing yourself, for ever raking over the ashes of the past and unable to look to the future.

This hardly requires an answer, because it is so obviously an expression of fear at losing control. Tough people have to invest a great deal of their time and energy and space in defending themselves against their own feelings. They have been taught that big boys do not cry, that to feel fear is to become weak. They are scared of any situation where they might show their feelings, and therapy is obviously threatening to them. Fortunately, tough people cannot keep it up the whole time, and many of them sooner or later are likely to need help and to have the insight to see this for themselves.

More serious, however, is the myth that therapy is only for people who are mentally ill – and a more subtle version of this which sees therapy as basically for nutters, but quite good for temporary clients. For example, it is widely supposed that you have to have a 'real' problem to need help from one of the therapies. That is to say, you have to be temporarily unhinged or completely unable to cope. So when counselling is offered to people caught up in a major disaster, such as the King's Cross underground fire, or the Zeebrugge ferry tragedy, many of us smugly think that the therapy is for the grief or the shock, rather than for the person. In fact it is for the person, and not for the grief or shock. It is a mistake to think that therapy starts with the assumption that a person and his or her feelings are somehow separate. When we have problems we have them as ourselves – they are not tacked on to us like some appendix that can be neatly cut out and taken away, making us well again.

It is happening here

In spite of all the scepticism that undoubtedly is around, more and more people are receiving personal help from therapists. Those who are going into therapy really are ordinary people. They are not fashionable eccentrics, self-indulgent yuppies, nor simply the innocent victims of occasional tragedy. It seems much more likely that the clients who are turning to counselling and other forms of therapy in their millions can only be ordinary people, people who have the same ordinary problems and common-place unhappinesses that have been around for centuries. Until fairly recently therapy was not available in a form which they could use or afford, and now that it is, more people are facing up to the unpleasant facts of their lives and trying to do something about them. They have come to recognise by many different routes that they do not need simply to sit back and suffer, to accept a quality of life which is not good enough. So they have plucked up their courage and asked for help.

For them therapy is definitely not a medical treatment. It is a positive health-giving activity, designed to enhance their lives in every direction.

3　Starting point for therapy

Problems

The starting point for most people is that they see themselves as having a problem of some kind. We asked one counsellor who is also a psychotherapist – and who wished to remain anonymous so that none of her clients could be identified – to list for us the reasons people gave for seeing her in the first place. She told us about her most recent thirty clients, of whom she had taken on twenty-two for counselling and eight for psychotherapy. She added that she had no way of checking how typical they were generally, but believed that it was 'unlikely they were untypical' of her practice over the last five years.

The counselling clients were overwhelmingly concerned about personal relationships. Ten of them began by presenting some aspect of marriage or its equivalent as a problem, and she added that three of these were in violent marriages, five were seriously considering divorce but had made no official moves about it, and two had felt unable to cope when their partners had had affairs. There had been three clients who started by referring to problems with their children, and six whose opening statements in counselling were about parents. This left three from the original twenty-two, of whom two could be said to be in a very similar category, since they began by talking about a recent bereavement. One client had said that she wanted to stop being over-weight, and went on fairly quickly to say that her main problem was her husband.

In giving us these figures, our informant emphasised that she had done strictly what we asked, and only looked at the opening problem. In all the cases she referred to, the clients had fairly quickly added information which showed that the problem was much more complex, but it always involved some aspect of the client's relationships with other people, and the effect this had on their perception of themselves. Most said they felt they were to blame in some way. Eight of them were men, and fourteen were women.

The eight clients who came into psychotherapy included two who had previously been in counselling with her. None of the eight, however, was working to solve specific problems – this, she said, was not the way psychotherapy worked. They were mainly concerned with issues that went back to childhood experience – issues which affected them today in their roles as parent, spouse, boss or worker. Each in their own way lacked the confidence to be fully themselves. Most had decided to go into psychotherapy as a result of some kind of crisis or series of crises which they felt unable to resolve for themselves without better self-understanding.

First step

The part crisis plays in making people consider therapy is important. The first step in dealing with any problem is to realise that you have one. Yet this is much more easily said than done unless there is a crisis. Why is it so difficult?

For example, why is it that somebody can feel very unhappy with a marriage for year after year, and still be quite surprised when other people suggest they should do something constructive about it? Why is it that a person might have a succession of poorly paid jobs which he or she keeps losing, and yet regards this merely as a chapter of accidents or a run of bad luck, instead of seeing it as a sign of something very wrong which needs to be changed? Why is it that you or I might eat all the things which are bad for us when we are unhappy – cheering ourselves up in the worst possible way for our own health? Or maybe what we do is drink or smoke too much, or work too hard, or never enjoy life – and still cannot see that this is a problem we need to tackle now, instead of putting it off yet again. Why is it that we can become so aware that life is not any fun, and yet not see that this is a problem we could place on the top of our agenda?

The fact is that millions of us live with problems we do not recognise as 'real' problems. In many cases the main reason we do this is that we are quite prepared to put up with a relatively low quality of life. We do not expect our marriages or our jobs or our relationships to be very fulfilling. The idea that we might be a lot happier most of the time seems absurd. So we put up with the anger and the fear and think of ourselves not as angry or fearful people, but as being a bit frustrated or having a few worries. We split off the unhappy part of us and try to forget it. Usually this works, and we can cope. For some reason we seem to think that a problem is not a real problem if we can cope with it.

Coping is something most of us know a lot about. Indeed, it is still a central part of the general philosophy of life these days, as it has been for centuries, even though – as we have seen – things are changing now. For a lot of us it still takes quite a leap of the imagination to recognise that coping is not good enough – that we are worth better than this. Many of us are not at all used to thinking of ourselves as deserving happiness and fulfilment. We do not have such a high opinion of ourselves. Happiness seems to us to be a matter of chance – indeed, that is where the word comes from. Fulfilment is something that other people experience, not us. We cope with the lack of these things in the same way that we put up with miserable weather – because it is there, because it happens, because we believe we can do nothing to change it. Maybe we cannot do anything about the weather, but usually we can do something to improve our own happiness and fulfilment.

This does not apply to everybody, naturally. There are many people who believe that life is what you make it. They regard happiness and fulfilment as something you have to achieve through hard work. Nevertheless, it cannot be achieved all the time, and when it becomes elusive and no amount of hard work seems to make any difference they begin to think that this is because they are failing personally in some way. For them, coping tends to mean keeping quiet about a sense of personal inadequacy, weakness, and lack of attainment.

Short-term advantages

Whatever our attitude to life in general, there are, of course, many short-term advantages in being able to cope. For a start, it seems better than being unable to cope. That would mean giving in to the misery, resigning from the battle, and, we fear, becoming a casualty. If we stopped coping things would get worse and we would be overwhelmed by our problems. Worse still, we would become dependent on other people in a way which might be quite unacceptable.

Many of us live with people at home or at work who make it quite clear that any failure to cope on our part will result in massive anger and rejection from them. They would have to pick up the pieces, and they are not likely to thank us for it. They may even make us pay for it – indeed, this is more than likely. Many of us also know only too well that if we fail to cope, those closest to us will suffer, and we shall feel responsible.

It isn't surprising then that when we feel we are losing we do our best to cope. If we can tell ourselves that our problems are not really as big as they seem, if we can deny that they exist, or pretend that they are not really anybody's fault, but just happening, like the weather, then we feel safer. There are plenty of people who seem ready to help us use this strategy. They are very keen for us to put our troubles behind us, where we cannot see them even if they are still there, because they do not want us to make them feel as unhappy as we do. If you want to bottle up your problems there will never be a shortage of people willing to help you do this.

Crisis

Problems and difficulties which are swept under the carpet are still there, and in time they mount up and produce a crisis. It often takes a catastrophe of some sort to teach us that we need help, that unless we find somebody we can depend on, if only for a while, we are going to end up in worse trouble. This is a pity, but it's nevertheless true.

Although we are unlikely to think so at the time, a major crisis in our lives can help us become much happier, more fulfilled people. It has become a cliché, but the fact is that we can often look back at turning points in our life and recognise that what seemed terrible at the time was probably one of the best things that could have happened to us. Catastrophe forces us into making changes we had resisted previously. It makes us strip away the scaffolding of compromise which props up so many of our derelict relationships, and for a while, everything seems to be falling on top of us. But when the dust clears we have a chance to build something new for ourselves.

None of this comes easily. At first all we know is that things will have to change, that we need help because we cannot any longer manage by ourselves. However, the people closest to us may be the last people we can turn to. We may recognise eventually that we have a 'real' problem, but we do not always know what to do about it.

Resistance to therapy

A major reason why people do not ask for help even at this point, when they begin to recognise they need it, is that they meet resistance from people close to them. In marriage, for example, the unhappy partner who wants to ask for help is quite likely to be discouraged from seeking it by the other partner. All sorts of reasons may be given – that there really isn't anything wrong and too much fuss is being made about nothing, that things will get better soon, that asking for help will be an admission of failure, that nothing is wrong that couldn't be put right by a little more sex and more money, or a little less sex and more money. When you say you need help from an outsider you are often seen as accusing the other person of being a failure, particularly in those marriages which began with the intention of making one another happy. The idea of failure in marriage as the worst thing that can happen to an adult is still very widespread, and being unhappy counts as failure in a great many marriages.

Resistance to seeking therapy can also come from some official sources. There are still, for example, many general practitioners who are more willing to reach for the prescription pad when a patient is depressed or anxious than to listen themselves or recommend somebody who is trained to listen. It is true that many more GPs' practices these days employ a counsellor or have a list of psychotherapists the doctors recommend, but most still do not, and this can scarcely be explained by simple ignorance. It is much more likely to be some kind of passive resistance to the idea. Doctors are human too, and no more immune than the rest of us to the philosophy of coping.

Much the same applies to the churches – the other traditional source of help in time of need. Religious organisations have been at the forefront of the growth of the counselling and psychotherapy movement, yet there are still many parishes where help will not be given. Also, certain religious groups are widely known to have dogmatic views on some issues – unwanted pregnancy, marital breakdown, extra-marital affairs, suicidal feelings and so on. There does not seem to be much point in going to them for help if you already know what they will say.

To sum up, recognising that we need help is difficult in itself, and when we do begin to accept the fact, we may well find that the people who say they care about us, or whom we expect to support us, may not do so.

It takes courage

The one thing we need most while we try to decide whether or not to seek help is courage. We have to hang on to the belief that we are worthy of help, and all the times throughout our lives that we have been discouraged from thinking such thoughts stand like an army in our path, blocking the way, waving slogans and shouting excuses at us.

Some of the slogans and excuses are about fear of change. Maybe we feel bad now, but we have a lot to be thankful for, we say. Maybe stirring things up will make them worse. Maybe if we tamper with such things we will run the risk of going mad. It is natural to be afraid of change, and we have no real way of knowing that the people we might go to for help will understand and accept this.

Some of our excuses arise from a fear of selfishness. To spend time and money on counselling, psychotherapy, or analysis is to spend it on ourselves. We say we cannot afford it, or give in too easily when other people tell us we cannot or should not. Or we feel uncomfortable with the thought of having something for ourselves because we are not used to this. There are many of us who are afraid of turning into self-indulgent, selfish people who could manage to live without making endless sacrifices for others. We are afraid of being ungrateful and inconsiderate, and asking for help would be evidence of a lack of gratitude for all that had been done for us.

There is also the fear of the stigma attached to asking for help from people associated with psychology or psychiatry. According to the Sunday supplements it may now be just about fashionable in certain middle-class circles to swap stories about visits to one's psychotherapist. It is far from being like this for the vast majority of people. Going regularly to see a counsellor or psychotherapist is still regarded by a great many people as evidence of mental instability, psychiatric illness, or straightforward lunacy. So those who go tend not to talk about it except to people who admit they have also been.

We have no way of knowing how many people are put off from going for counselling or psychotherapy by the fear of being regarded as inadequate, but there are grounds for suspecting that there is a considerable number. Certainly this is a reaction commonly found by managers who are trained in counselling skills and offer their services to other employees as part of a confidential company counselling service. It is also quite common for colleges or universities to offer psychotherapy to all who want it, but to call it counselling because people are afraid of the stigma attached to receiving psychotherapy.

We can also be afraid and frustrated because of sheer exhaustion. We can feel simply too tired out to want to do anything about problems and unhappiness. There does not seem to be any point in bothering. This can happen when we have experienced so many losses in life that our whole commitment to going on has become weakened, and we suspect that our problems are beyond repair. The effort of living seems to be just too much.

Accepting the need

So for nearly all of us, courage is required not only to accept that we need help from a stranger, but also to risk the anger or rejection of people who are threatened by our need to ask for such help. What makes the difference between only thinking we need help and actually going to ask for it is not that we despair, that we come to the end of our tether, or lose all hope and confidence, as many of the sceptics and scorners would have us believe, but quite the reverse. We may well have hit a crisis before we decide to act, but even this is not quite enough. For a variety of reasons we find within ourselves the resources we need to be able to afford a ray of hope.

Often all that happens is that we meet a stranger or an acquaintance who is honest enough to recognise and acknowledge our need for help, and who knows that such help is available. Sometimes we see other people being happier than we are at moments when we are resting from the battle and have the energy to look clearly at ourselves. Or maybe we are granted the space in a busy life quite by chance to take stock and face the facts of our life.

Crisis, catastrophe, together with the insight we need if we are to stand back and look at ourselves open the door for us into a world of change. They increase our chances of being able to look back one day and say that although things were dreadful then, we would not have done anything about our deepest needs if it hadn't been for the fact that we admitted our need for help. We would have carried our problems as 'luggage' around forever.

Inside many of us are uncompleted tasks from the past – grieving we have never felt safe enough to complete, needless guilt which we carry wherever we go, not recognising that it is an unnecessary burden; apparently unbreakable rules of life which restrict our happiness, but which we blindly obey long after the need for them has disappeared. These constitute the luggage which we take with us into psychotherapy or analysis or counselling as we begin the journey into change, led by the glimmer of hope that there is something better for us, and that we deserve it.

4 People in therapy

Ourselves

Are you the sort of person who could benefit from going to see a counsellor, psychotherapist, or analyst? One way to find out is to ask a few of the people who are already in therapy about why they started. What sort of people are they, and why do they go?

In our research for this book we interviewed many people who had done so. The following accounts are adapted from transcripts made in interviews with people who seemed typical of the bulk of these interviewees. We have altered the names and a few of the less important facts about them in order to disguise their identities. The words are their own.

Peter

Peter is in his mid-twenties, left school at sixteen, and worked in a bank where he discovered he had a natural aptitude for computers. He now works as a technician for a bank and is married to Julie. The two of them go to see a psychotherapist together once a week.

I didn't see any need for it at the start.

It was Julie who insisted we should both go. She went for counselling first, because she was unhappy with our marriage, and then started to insist that either I should go with her or find somebody to go to myself. It was either that or she was leaving. I was quite happy with the marriage, but I didn't want to end up with a divorce for no reason so I went along. The fact is, once we started the counselling, I began to realise that I had been unhappy for a long time, but simply didn't want to admit it to myself. You don't always recognise it when things are going wrong. You blame the other person, or put it down to stress at work and feeling tired, or just muddle through and say to yourself, that's Julie – the kind of person she is, never very happy, always worrying about something going wrong. All the time, though, it was just as much me as her.

Peter is representative of a great many clients – the partners of people who seek help, but who are slow to recognise their own need. Why had it taken him so long?

There are lots of reasons. Image is one – I didn't see myself as somebody who goes to a shrink, I suppose. I was brought up to be self-sufficient, not to go running for help just because of unhappiness, and not to blab about my private affairs in front of strangers. I was afraid of it getting out at work, too. I could take the ragging from my mates, but where I work it can be a black mark against you if you are seen as not coping with your private life – even though most of us in the team seem to be always facing some kind of crisis at home. Two of them are divorced, and I know for a fact that three are having affairs on the side, and one of those has a young family. I was furious with Julie when she pushed me into going. Now I think it's the best thing that ever happened in our marriage.

The best thing?

Yes. The best thing. We're working on it together, and facing up to how difficult it really is to be fair to each other and make a go of it. I thought we could manage that without help, but we couldn't, and I really believe that we aren't all that different from everybody else.

Sarah

Sarah represents another group, the clients and patients whose lives were disrupted by a major crisis. In her case it was a sudden, dramatic, devastating bereavement. She is a secretary in her forties, and has a ten-year-old son. She was married first at 22, divorced 10 years later, and then met and married Geoff. He died in a car accident last year. She began therapy six months later.

When Geoff was killed, I thought it was the end of me. I kept saying over and over in my head that this was bound to happen, that you can't ever be really happy for long, that my last chance had gone now, and I might as well die. I got through the funeral, and people kept saying they hoped I wouldn't do anything stupid, and to think of my son, Michael, and all the time I was making my mind up to die. I made all sorts of plans, carefully and rationally. But even that kept going wrong. My work got steadily worse, and in the end I was told in no uncertain terms by my boss to go and see my doctor and tell her. She was marvellous. I was in there for two hours, crying my eyes out for the first time since the accident. I thought she would just give me pills but she didn't. She listened. Then she recommended somebody at the hospital, a psychotherapist. Now I go twice a week for an hour each time. I still feel dreadful, but at least now I can talk about it and cry. Michael and I talk about Geoff, too, and I know that's important. I still think about suicide, but not so often.

Philip

Philip's friends 'thought he had it made'. He was attractive, 32 years old, with a good job as an engineer, and a roomy flat in the best part of town. He played cricket and golf in the summer, rugby in the winter, squash all year round. He was also single, and played the field. 'My affairs were legendary,' he said.

So what went wrong? He just wasn't happy.

I got round to thinking that I wasn't getting anything really good out of life. I had plenty of company, lots to do, and I could always keep myself busy. Most of the time, though, that's all I was doing, keeping busy. I caught myself one day making conversation for the umpteenth time with somebody I had just met, and realised that I never actually talked to anybody. I could chat people up, tell jokes, say all the right things, but none of it was leading anywhere, just filling in time.

It was an important moment for him. A week or so earlier he had reached the end of an affair with a married woman who had decided to try to make her marriage work. 'Will you miss me?' he had asked. 'I don't suppose so,' she told him. 'It was fun, but nothing substantial.' It was a cruel thing to say, and it hurt. But Philip shrugged it off, and started to look around for the next affair.

I couldn't get those words out of my mind. I hated her for it. It made me feel trivial. Looking back now, though, I can see that she did me a favour. It made me stop and think about things like I never had before. I kept asking myself – what did she mean? How could she say that to me?

Then he began to understand why, or at least to see some truth in it for himself.

It was me and my life that was insubstantial.

My work was well-paid but getting nowhere. My flat was nice, but it was empty. I had no family, no real friends. All I had was my image with the lads, their fantasies about me that I felt I had to live up to. Well, I couldn't have said any of this three years ago when I first went into therapy. I just felt uneasy and miserable, and lonely. I was trapped and I didn't know why. I don't need those feelings now. I'm changing.

How does this show?

You'd have to have known me then to see the difference. My confidence in myself is much more certain for one thing, and I've become more serious about life without, I hope, losing my sense of fun. I'm still stuck as far as my job's concerned, but I'm probably going to start my own business next year, depending on one or two things coming out right this year. I don't know how it shows. I just feel better. I'm changing for the better, growing up. But it's been a painful and difficult business.

You could see what he meant. Listening to him, looking at him, it was hard to imagine the Philip he had described, the Philip he had been three years ago.

Kathy

Kathy is training to be a counsellor, and hopes later to go on to psychotherapy training. Her present course takes up one evening a week and lasts three years. During the day she teaches at a school in Edinburgh.
   Is it because she wants to be a psychotherapist herself that she is in therapy as a client?

That's not the only reason, though of course, everybody who wants to practise full-time, as I do one day, really needs to be in therapy. You need to understand everything you can about yourself, and to be able to know what it's like to be on the receiving end. But that's not why I started in the first place.

What happened?

Well, it's a long story but I suppose the nub of it is that I've spent most of my life feeling depressed and inadequate. The worst time was at college when I was desperately unhappy and quite often suicidal. For two years I saw a psychiatrist on an out-patient basis and lived on tranquilizers and anti-depressants. These had horrible side-effects and I would swing between being a zombie and a nervous wreck. After taking my finals I recovered from the worst feeling of depression but it was never far away, holding me back from real happiness and fulfilment.
   I also became trapped in a pattern of relating to men, though I wasn't aware of it for many years. I would get involved with a man because I needed someone and he happened to be around and willing. I never made a choice about whether he was the kind of person I really found attractive or wanted to have a relationship with. I'd go into the thing blindly, seducing them by being helpless and vulnerable. I would then try to live up to being the kind of person they expected, performing unbelievable contortions to make the relationship work. You see, part of me was strong and intelligent but very frightened, hence this flight into dependency. Each time I ended up being angry

with them for not being the kind of person I really wanted and angry with myself for giving up my initiative and self-respect. Eventually I would withdraw from anything intimate – touching, cuddling, making love – and it would always end up looking as though my problem was a sexual one.

Over a period of about ten years, Kathy had three serious relationships where this happened, and many more that were short-lived and casual. She tried to get help with her depression and she also read about the subject for herself.

Since college I had always thought of myself as having a problem with 'depression' but never dreamt that this might be connected with my difficulties in relationships. I began to think I was the sort of person who would never have a really fulfilling relationship.

Bit by bit, however, I began to be able to stand back and look at myself. I can see now that through all those years I was a very angry person inside, hating to be dependent on people and quite unable to tell them about what I wanted and needed. Of course nothing would go right for me with all that anger inside, festering away, and distorting my expectations of life. It's only now that I am beginning to understand my anger and accept it, that I can get it into proportion and start to relate honestly with people.

And the therapy?

It took a long time to find the right therapist. I go to see her once a week. She's a gem.

PART II
USES OF THERAPY

5   Better than advice

It is now time to look at the difference between the three
therapies. What we would really like to do is define each one of
them in a water-tight way, and say: right – that's what
counselling is, and that's what psychotherapy is, and that's what
analysis is, and now you know the difference between them. We
would also like to be able to say: if you want this kind of thing
you should always see a counsellor; if it's this sort of thing, go
into psychotherapy; and if this is what you want go for analysis.

But it isn't as simple as that, so we can't – and we haven't
met anybody in our research for this book who could do it
either. There isn't any hard and fast rule. What we can do,
however, is give you a rough idea over the next three chapters
of what the differences are, what each kind of therapy is for,
and the sort of territory it covers.

Back to basics first. A good way to start – even at the risk of
being simplistic – is by looking at the whole notion of advice.
Let us invent somebody called James and suppose that he is
worried about a problem and decides to talk about it with a
friend in order to get some advice.

James will probably try to choose somebody whom he thinks
of as a good, sympathetic listener. He goes to see such a friend,
says he wants help, and begins to talk. The friend nods, and
says *hmm* in the right places, and tries hard to understand
James' problem. From time to time he interrupts and asks a
question. Eventually, he thinks he has understood what's
wrong, and checks with James. 'Let me see if I've got it
right . . .' he says, and tells James what he thinks James has
said. 'Yes,' says James. 'That's it. That's exactly what's
bothering me.' 'Right,' says the friend, 'then here's what you
have to do . . .' And he gives his advice.

Nothing wrong with that, you might think. Wouldn't it be
nice if we could all do it? Or would it?

The point is that if you go to see a professional counsellor, psychotherapist, or analyst, this is not what is likely to happen. Generally speaking, they do not see their job as being to listen sympathetically and then give advice. Most of them will avoid it like the plague. They try to do something rather more useful than this.

What's wrong with advice

Suppose James had come to you. Would you really listen? Unless you've been trained as a listener, the answer is, probably not.

Listening to somebody, however carefully, in order to identify the other person's problem and then come up with some answers is a deceptive business. From the start you are working towards that moment when an idea will form in your head as to what is wrong. Sooner or later you begin to get the idea, and when you think this is correct and the evidence mounts up in its favour, you begin to stop listening to anything which might go against it or which seems irrelevant and might side-track you. For example, you might think James is rambling on a bit or exaggerating and this can be a bit frustrating.

Very soon all the questions you ask are designed to keep him 'talking to the point' – which means making sure he is working on the same lines as you, even if you have to argue with him about this by telling him that what he is saying is not what he is really saying, or bully him a little by telling him to shut up for a minute and listen to you. You stop listening to the bits which you think don't matter, and pretty soon you stop listening altogether.

The sooner this happens, the better! After all, when you really understand the problem there isn't any point in wasting the other person's time by listening to him any more, because now you can give the advice he wants.

But is this really what he wants? Probably not. There are times we want to be listened to for the sake of being listened to. Asking for advice is more often than not just an excuse for this.

We all need attention and acknowledgement and the feeling that people are interested in us for ourselves and not just in our problems. Because this is not an easy thing to ask for straight out, we dress it up as a request for advice. Unfortunately this usually means we do not get listened to the way we want.

And even if we really do want advice, what we get is bound to be a bit suspect. It generally says a lot more about the experiences and needs of the adviser than those of the person being advised. That is why people who give advice say things like: 'If I were you' – which is impossible, because they never can be you. Or, 'What I would do is this . . .' when it won't be them that has to do it. Or, 'exactly the same thing happened to me' – when nothing that happens to anybody is exactly the same thing that happens to somebody else.

Not surprisingly, people seldom take advice even when they have asked for it. We really need to be a bit sceptical about the value of advice itself and therefore about the value of giving it and asking for it. If you were a professional, giving out advice all day, surely you would get sceptical too.

Meeting as equals

If this is not enough to put you off advice, then consider the relationship between the adviser and the person who gets the advice. The two never really meet as equals. That is to say, James will tend to go to somebody whom he looks up to in some way, whose experience of life, it seems to James, is in some sense more valuable than James' own experience. Well, so it might be. But the effect on James is that it encourages him to think of himself as relatively inferior. The effect on his friend is that it encourages him to feel superior. It is flattering to be asked for advice, and this is why. What might help James even more is to feel that his own experience is just as valuable as anybody else's. The relationship which is set up when people give advice is always to some extent based on the devaluation of the person asking for advice.

With a good adviser, and if James gets along fine without advice most of the time, this may not matter very much. But if you are the adviser, and you see lots of people every day who flatter you in this way, it can have the long-term effect of making you feel superior most of the time. You end up having a vested interest in people like James knocking on your door and being dependent on you. Before long you are saying things like, 'Most people just want to be told what to do,' and 'All most people need is a good kick up the backside and being told to get on with it.' That's bad for them, and it's bad for you. So professional helpers try to avoid it happening, and are very reluctant to be turned into advisers.

Something better

There is another reason why counsellors, psychotherapists and
analysts are chary of being turned into advisers. If they only
listen to the *presenting* problem – the one which James begins
by describing – they may miss completely the problem
underneath which is more important to him. For example, if he
wants sympathy and not advice, then this might mean that
James is lonely, or that he lacks self-confidence, or that he has
never in all his life thought that anybody would really want to
know how he truly felt.

So they take the view that it is safer for James, and safer for
them, to give him at least the opportunity to go a bit deeper
and talk about his feelings just in case the presenting problem
is not the real problem. What's more, they say, it hardly ever *is*
the real problem.

Listening with empathy

Of course, this brings a new dimension into the listening. For
one thing, sympathy is not enough – it might even be
positively harmful. For example, suppose James is lonely
because his mother died last year, and he hasn't felt able to
make any new friends since. Sympathy would mean saying
things like 'I'm sorry,' and 'You must miss her.' But for all we
know, James might have been furious with his mother. He
might not be sorry in the conventional sense, and who are we
to tell him, in effect, that he *has to* miss her? Such normal
expressions of sympathy would not encourage him to talk
about any of his true feelings. Sympathy could mean that he
simply writes us off as people who do not want to understand.
He might feel that nobody will ever understand and become
even more desperate and isolated, heading for a major
breakdown.

A good therapist – counsellor, psychotherapist or analyst –
would try to enable James to feel safe enough to show how he
feels. Then the therapist would listen as if this feeling –
whatever it is – belonged at that moment to the two of them.
This is roughly what is meant by 'empathy'.

Therapists listen with empathy, not sympathy. They keep
quiet and tune in with their own feelings, doing all they can to
see the world the way their clients see it, to feel what they feel
right now and right here. It also means they do not make moral
judgements about what is said, because that stops them feeling
the same as their clients, and also stops their clients from

feeling safe, driving the problem underground again. What is said has to be kept as confidential between them for the same reason.

More useful than advice

All the professional ways of helping, then, are attempts to improve on the traditional advice methods. We have looked at some of the reasons for this, but there are others too which are just as important.

What about James' experience when he asked for advice, for example? He was extraordinarily lucky. Most people are not nearly so patient. 'You think you've got a problem!' they might say. 'You should hear what happened to me . . .' And they hijack the conversation which you thought would be about you, and turn it into a conversation about them. Or they ask long and involved questions not because they want to help but because they feel better for knowing you feel worse. Or they listen because later on they want to tell somebody else about your problems and have fun gossiping. Or they get furious if you don't take their advice. Good professional therapists do not do any of these things.

Traditionally people used to turn to a member of their family for advice, but this can be risky. However much they love you (and this might not be very much at all), they tend to have fixed ideas about you, and to feel threatened if you look like turning into somebody they cannot understand. So their ways of listening and of giving advice tend to meet their needs first, and your own needs last. This often happens with close friends, and with colleagues too. Even if it doesn't happen, and you know people who will want to help, you may have good reasons for not wanting to burden them with your troubles. They might have enough on their plate already. None of this need apply to a professional helper.

The need for change

But the most important point we can make about advice has not been made yet. It is that people who ask for advice about a problem have to have one in the first place, and this means they have to see it as if it were an object in itself. In other words they regard their problems as in some way separate from them, tacked on to their life, rather than a product of the kind of people they are.

The fact is, the kinds of problems we have, and the ways in

which we have them, are completely characteristic of us. Our problems are an integral part of who we are. We may be able to separate the two things mentally, but this is just a trick of the mind, an illusion we find convenient or comforting.

This is important because it means that very often we cannot actually gain a lot from solving problems one by one in isolation. All we shall manage to do is solve them in one form, only to come up against the same problem a short time later in another guise. This short-term relief may be what we are looking for, of course, and if that is all we want, fine. But on a longer-term basis there is something better, and that is to solve our problems in such a way that we also increase our capacity for not having problems – and that means changing ourselves in some way.

Some people with problems think that this is unnecessary; others that it might be necessary but is totally impossible. For example, they might say they are too old to change, or that you are stuck with what you are because nobody can change his or her personality. Nevertheless there are plenty of people who come round to the belief that personal change is not only possible but vitally necessary. They want to have fewer problems, not just get better at solving them.

This leads to one of the major differences between counselling, psychotherapy, and analysis. Counselling, unlike the other two, tends to be thought of as the right way to help people who are not looking to change who they are, but wish to concentrate on solving problems without undergoing deep personal change.

6 Three kinds of therapy

Counselling

As we have already seen, receiving counselling means being listened to with empathy so that you can express how you feel in order to begin to find your own solutions to problems. It does not mean being given sympathy in the conventional sense, it does not mean being listened to so somebody can tell you what they would do, and it does not mean being judged on moral or other grounds by somebody who might not accept you. The counsellor is always on your side, whatever you have done, and whatever feelings you express.

Because of this, being listened to by a counsellor when you feel troubled can be quite enough to help you feel better, so you can actually go away able to do what you knew all along in your heart you had to do. This point needs a little more explanation.

Most of us grow steadily isolated when we have frustrations or worries. We begin to feel as though nobody else can possibly understand, that there is nobody who will know how we feel, or maybe that it is all our fault – we must have done something to deserve it. Being listened to the right way helps us put such feelings into proportion. We find we can face up to issues more easily and take responsiblity for our part in them, as well as seeing more clearly what other people may be doing to us. We can get the anger out, or talk safely about our fears. We can look at the alternatives and weigh them up more rationally. While we are doing this in private with a therapist the people who might be shocked or threatened by what is in our hearts are not there to shut us up. We have room to talk, room to be listened to. All this helps us to see what we need to do next, and encourages us to go ahead and do it.

Nevertheless this takes a lot of skill and hard work on the

part of the counsellor. It requires a trained listener who is aware of his or her own needs and problems, and who will try not to let these become the issue when you work with him or her. Counsellors learn in their training how to listen intently, how to see things the way you see them, how to help you test out various possible solutions, and how to enable you to go a bit deeper when you need to, without feeling too threatened. Their main aim is to reach the point where you feel you can manage by yourself without help from people like them.

Psychotherapy

Psychotherapy, on the other hand, is very much about change. It aims to get much more to the roots of your problems and to enable you to begin to see how they are connected so you can change into the kind of person who has fewer problems and much more choice in life.

When you work with a psychotherapist it is quite likely that you will spend most of the time exploring the connections not only between the various problems you have, but also between other aspects of your experience of being a person. Quite often this will mean talking about things that happened long ago in childhood, so that you can begin to understand the way your relationships in the family, particularly with your parents, are affecting you right now. Events which still hurt from those days which you can recall vividly are looked at again, because in understanding them afresh you can begin to build a new picture of yourself. From time to time, what you remember will not be enough, because it will not in itself explain the way you feel. There will be parts missing from the jigsaw puzzle, because you find them too painful to recall. Psychotherapy can enable you to open up such suppressed memories, so that more of your experience becomes positively valuable to you.

This requires just as much training, hard work and skill on the part of the psychotherapist as a counsellor needs – some people would say it takes even more. There are going to be many times in carrying out such a task when the therapist will use not just practical knowledge of you and what you say but also theoretical knowledge of the way we become people. For example, there is the notion we have just used, that memories of very disturbing events get suppressed, and the similar idea that when a memory has been lost it is probably because it relates to an incident that is still too painful to remember.

These ideas – the theoretical basis of psychotherapy – may in some cases be very precise, rather like a detailed map, and in other instances they may be sketchy and tentative. They belong to three different traditions, too, the 'psycho-dynamic' tradition which is most commonly linked with Freud, Jung, and their followers, the 'existential-humanistic' tradition, which is based on a different – some would say, more optimistic – view of mankind, and the 'behavioural' tradition which has been built on discoveries made in experimental psychology since the 1920s, and which tends also to be anti-Freudian in some important respects. However, as we shall see later, these categories can only be regarded as a very loose and imperfect way of looking at the rich variety of ideas which inform psychotherapy, and, indeed, therapy generally.

Psychotherapy also demands more commitment from the client or patient than counselling usually does, apart from anything else because there will be a great deal of territory to explore in order to find the most useful connections. The time required to do this is such that where a counsellor might see somebody for only a few sessions at irregularly spaced intervals over a period of several months or even less, a psychotherapist would normally expect to see the client once or twice a week for exactly fifty minutes a session, over a period of two to three years.

Incidentally, whether you will be called a client or a patient when you go to see a psychotherapist depends very much on the practitioner.

Analysis

Analysis is also designed to bring about change, and is generally thought of as being an attempt to bring about the most thorough and radical change of all – what most ordinary people would regard as a change of personality. It has been called the 'Rolls Royce' of the therapy movement.

The commitment required is four or five days per week with the analyst, each time for a fifty minute session, and the process goes on for at least three years in most cases, and often for longer than that. You might say that in comparison with psychotherapy which tries to get at the roots of the problem, analysis tries to get at the roots of the roots.

What the client (technically known in this kind of therapy as the 'analysand') and the analyst are trying to do is also about connections. The extra time that is available means that in principle it should be possible to explore all the ways a person has of being what he or she is, more widely, more deeply, and with less concern for objectives. That is to say, it can be done for its own sake, free of the constraints and pressures which are inevitably imposed by having some kind of goal or purpose beyond this. To give you an analogy, it is more like pure science than applied science.

Compared with other approaches to therapy, much more of the suppressed material that is inside us – the 'unconscious' mind – can be explored and made conscious to the analysand. This can be tackled by looking at dreams and exploring the logic that lies behind their apparent lack of logic. Also, the use of a method called 'free association', in which the analysand is encouraged to say anything that comes into his or her mind without holding back any feelings, means that nothing in the world of the analysand need be excluded. Of course, this method can also be used in psychotherapy and counselling, but it can go much further in analysis because there is time and space to follow it wherever it may lead.

Analysis is important in another way, too. Since the early beginnings of what we have called the therapy movement, this has been where a great deal of the most important theoretical work has been done. The intensive nature of analysis, the fact that it need not be rushed, and the fascination such work holds for people who are interested in the nature of human experience and development are some of the reasons why. In historical terms, psychotherapy and counselling, however they are practised and whether or not they belong to the psycho-dynamic tradition, owe a great debt to psychoanalysis. It is still the most important method of enabling the practitioners of therapy to know themselves thoroughly enough to reduce the risk to their own clients as far as this may knowingly be reduced. All analysts have to be analysed themselves to qualify, and the experience of a full analysis lasting several years is an important and highly regarded element in the training of many psychotherapists. Indeed, several analysts made the point when we interviewed them that most analysis these days is what is called 'training analysis'.

Not hard and fast

The Westminster Pastoral Foundation is one of the largest and most respected organisations in London providing counselling and psychotherapy. It also has offshoots in other parts of the UK. We asked its director, Derek Blows, what he thought the differences were.

First of all, therapy is a general term applying to any form of healing, and will include analysis. The distinction more commonly made is between analysis and psychotherapy and counselling. Again, there are no hard and fast definitions everyone is agreed on. You define the words to mean different things, or define them in a way that they overlap or coincide in some instances.

Generally speaking analysis is a word restricted to work done by the Jungians or Freudians who've had formal training in analytical societies and who see individuals four or five times a week. It goes on for a very long time and aims to really work with the unconscious in a very open-ended way, and in some cases aims for a considerable personality change. It doesn't always achieve it, but that's what it aims for. Psychotherapy on the other hand is usually used to mean forms of therapy derived from analysis and it implies the application of psychoanalytical principles in a more limited way. So you would see somebody for psychotherapy one to three times a week and probably for a less lengthy period. It wouldn't probe so deeply into the unconscious and it would probably be for a shorter period, but having said that, there is an overlap. People may well be doing in psychotherapy the same things as they would do in what is officially called analysis. And there is no rigid rule.

Yet it doesn't necessarily mean that people in psychotherapy work less intensively than those who are undergoing analysis.

They may actually be doing the same work. I mean it's possible. A colleague of mine who's very highly trained in analytic psychotherapy says that some of her once a week patients in hospital can work as intensively as some of her three or four times a week patients in private practice. A lot depends on the patients and where they are.

But do people who are in *counselling* work less intensively?

Well again, you see, it has many definitions. It can be used for a particular way of working, which is a way of responding, attending and listening to people and feeding back what you hear. Or it can be used in behavioural strategies in helping people and with a very considerable interventionist approach of the counsellor. Or you can use it for what is in effect analytic psychotherapy, where there are advantages in using the word 'counselling' because it's non-medical.

On the whole, a counsellor doesn't quite have the same medical associations in the popular mind that a psychotherapist does.

Schools and colleges, for example, prefer the description 'counselling' because many people might think that to see a psychotherapist means that you're mentally ill. 'Counselling' carries much less of a social stigma. Actually, the same person might practise counselling, psychotherapy and analysis, as I do myself.

So when he is in those three situations, is he aware of working in a very different way?

Yes and no. When I'm working as an analyst I know there's much more time. I don't have to be so active. I can wait. If I'm only seeing a person once a week I've got to be more on my toes, more active, as well as being prepared to let some things go. I may want to focus more on the presenting problem. A lot of psychotherapy is more concentrated on particular problems and one particular area whilst an analysis would be more likely to let it spread wherever it wants to go.

We put much the same questions to Jill Curtis. One of her most important roles in the British Association of Psychotherapists is to see the applicants first, and to decide what kind of help they need – such as analysis, psychotherapy, or counselling – before suggesting which therapist they should see. She gave us an example to illustrate the difference between a situation where counselling would probably be more useful than psychotherapy.

A man came to see me because his girlfriend had walked out on him and he was absolutely devastated. He found it quite impossible to think of other girl friends who had walked out on him – he didn't want to talk about that. He couldn't see that things that had happened at school had any bearing on this at all. He just wanted his girlfriend back and that was all there was to it. And that's what he wanted to talk about. He didn't want to tie things up because he didn't want to think about the future, he didn't want to think about the past. He just wanted someone to say, 'Yes – it must be awful to be on your own on a Sunday,' and what he wanted was about six or seven weeks of being able to do that and then sort of dust himself down and get on with his life. He didn't want to take the time, or he just wasn't in the situation where he wanted to understand what was happening. But he did need someone to talk to. And being told something like – well, why don't you go to the tennis club twice a week, and perhaps you could increase playing tennis – something like that. That was the kind of help he wanted.

What matters here is her last point: that was the kind of help he wanted. It was her job to find out what the client wanted, and she had completed this task. She was not implying that in wanting counselling rather than psychotherapy the man was disappointing her, or letting himself down, nor that he was in some way to be frowned at for not wanting to go deeper and explore the connections in his life which she could see between his early experience and his present-day difficulties. In every sense of the word, she respected him and his choice.

7 A choice of therapy

As we have seen, there is a considerable overlap between the three kinds of therapy, and there is also many variations within each type. We are now in a position to look at each of the three again, and suggest in more detail how you might find them useful. Here is how we are going to approach the exercise.

First, we shall look at the kinds of issues which people take into counselling so that you can get a better idea for yourself whether this might be of use to you or somebody you know. Secondly, we shall consider psychotherapy and analysis from the same perspective. Of course, this might be misleading, because as we have seen, not only is there an overlap, but also nobody just has problems which they take to a therapist to get solved. We take *ourselves* to the therapist, and our problems are a part of us. However, we shall leave you to correct the balance for yourself, bearing in mind what has already been said over the last two chapters about the differences between the three therapies.

The uses of counselling

Emergency problems
An important aspect of counselling is that, unlike either psychotherapy or analysis, it is often a one-session affair. In other words, if you arrange to see a therapist for counselling, it is generally acceptable for you to have just the one appointment, and maybe make another one at the end of that if you feel you need it. Because psychotherapy and analysis take very much longer, you book your time for these well in advance, and it is customary to see the therapist regularly on the same days each week and at the same time. There are also some counselling centres where you do not need even to call in

advance, but can just 'drop in', though this might only apply to certain days of the week between certain times, and these are usually advertised by the centre. Obviously, only a centre which has several counsellors can run a drop-in service, but more and more of them are trying to operate this way.

What this means in practice is that counselling is a good place to take emergency problems, particularly the sort that you have lived with for some time but which have quite suddenly come to a head or got out of control. Here are some real examples compiled from several different sources:

Ron: He came home from work a few days earlier to find that his wife had smashed up the kitchen and was a few doors away with a neighbour 'sobbing her eyes out' but refusing to see him. This made him angry, but it also frightened him because he did not really understand what it meant. She calmed down and came back home, and they patched things up. She said she didn't trust him any more, and had been unhappy for years. This, he said, was 'news to him'. He had nowhere else to turn, and came to see the counsellor in the hope that this would help him sort things out.

Dave: There had been a major row at home which Dave said had been brewing for some time. His mother was not speaking to him because he had become involved with a girl she did not approve of, and his father, who had been trying to ignore this, suddenly 'blew up' and told Dave to leave. Dave wanted to leave but had nowhere to go. He wanted to talk this over with the counsellor to see what to do next.

Mary: Married, with three young children, Mary was worried about her elderly mother who suffered from Alzheimer's disease and was in a nursing home. She visited every week, but her husband always refused to go with her, would not say why, and this was now getting too much for Mary. She wanted to talk about this to see if there was any way she could persuade him to give her more support with the problem.

Jana: Desperately worried about her school work and exams which were looming on the horizon, Jana was sure she would fail and let her parents down, but did not feel able to talk about this with them. That day a school friend had asked her to a party, and, when Jana said she had to work, had been very nasty to her. She said she needed help because she felt she was going out of her mind.

George: He was afraid he might be an alocholic, and wanted to know what he could do about this. He had been worried for some time, and came to the counselling centre on impulse because he happened to be going past on his way home.

Cynthia: Her teenage child had been staying out late far more than usual recently, and her husband had told Cynthia that this was her responsiblity. She wanted to talk about how she could be better at controlling her daughter.

Greg: When his parents were away, Greg had taken to dressing up in his mother's clothes, and he now did this most Saturdays, sometimes going out for walks dressed as a woman. He wanted to talk about what this might mean.

Frank: A widower for the last 10 years, 66-year-old Frank had been courting an attractive divorcee with a view to remarrying, but was worried about something an acquaintance had said about her past, and wanted to discuss this.

Other problem areas

Of course, problems do not have to be of the emergency kind to be worth seeing a counsellor about them. Other areas of difficulty in our lives often produce feelings of unhappiness that you cannot cope with. Counselling is a good way to begin to do something about these, particularly if you feel that there is nobody you already know who really understands the way you feel. Here are some examples:

Grief: the loss of any person, or of a pet, which results in you feeling that you cannot stop crying, that you might be to blame, that you should have got over it by now, that you would also like to be dead, that there isn't much point in going on, that you cannot enjoy your own life as a result of the loss. The loss need not be recent – these feelings can occur long afterwards, even many years. Nor do they have to be overwhelming – if they trouble you at all, counselling will probably be useful.

Violence: incidents of physical violence at home or at work or elsewhere in which you were attacked, or people around you were attacked, or you felt that you might get out of control and attack somebody else. The violence might be actual or threatened. Any situation in which you feel constantly belittled or bullied or cannot stop yourself wanting to do this to others is worth talking to a counsellor about. So is any incident where you have been the victim of a violent criminal act by somebody else.

If your job brings you into contact with violence, either deliberate or accidental, it is easy to underestimate the effect this can have on you. Any disturbing or unsettling feelings you have about such work can usefully be talked through with a counsellor.

Children: feelings of being unable to cope with babies, young or teenage children, fears of treating them badly or anger at their conduct, are often usefully discussed in counselling. Worries about their behaviour in and out of school, questions you wish to sort out in your mind which you may want to raise elsewhere (such as at the school or with a spouse) are also relevant. Any aspect of parenting can become a problem because none of us can be perfect parents. A counsellor will listen to how you feel and enable you to look for new options.

Sexual unhappiness: lack of communication about sex which is making you feel unhappy, or general lack of fulfilment with a regular partner is a good reason to see a counsellor. Shyness with members of the opposite sex is part of this too. Counselling may also be able to help you if you are unhappy about pregnancy or the lack of it, or if you are worried about your fertility or potency. If you are homosexual or bisexual, or suspect you might be, and have not told anybody who is important in your life or do not know what to do, a talk with a counsellor will be a good way to start tackling the issue for yourself.

Work: fears about losing your job, or any of the short- or long-term effects of unemployment can be discussed with a counsellor. Problems with relationships at work, fear of failure or feelings about lack of attainment, worries about stress, being stuck in a job you can do adequately, but dislike, fears about relocation, indeed all work worries can be usefully talked about in counselling.

Marriage: loss of faith or trust in a spouse, regrets about having married, lack of communication, major lack of agreement on starting a family, isolation and loneliness in marriage, worries about the health of a spouse – all these are usefully discussed in counselling. You do not have to see a marriage guidance counsellor first, and in any case the counsellor will want first of all to work with you as an individual, not as somebody else's other half. If you choose marriage guidance, this does not mean that the counsellor will be working to save the marriage unless both of you want it saved. Nor do you have to be legally married for a general counsellor or marriage guidance counsellor to agree to work with you.

Parents, siblings: family matters, such as disharmony or acrimony between parent and child or brothers and sisters can be a major source of unhappiness. All family problems which result in you not really knowing what to do – or, if you know, how to do it – can seem easier after counselling. This is often also the best way to begin to do something about worries concerning sexual behaviour in the family, such as incest or suspected incest, or the threat of incest.

Money: Generally speaking, counselling will not help you with a money problem in the sense that the counsellor will not lend you money. There are specialist agencies which concentrate on the problems of chronic debt or over-use of credit facilities, and you might get help from your local social security or social work departments. Nevertheless, if you are unhappy because of the lack of money and wish to talk this over, open to the possibility that the root cause of the problem is dependence on somebody else for money, or lack of communication with that person, counselling can be of benefit to you.

Addictions, compulsive behaviour: Addiction to alcohol, tobacco, drugs, medicaments such as tranquilizers, and addiction to gambling are probably not best dealt with by a general counsellor, but by specialists. You might save yourself some time by going direct to them, and your local library or citizens advice bureau will be the best place to start looking for their addresses. Some compulsive behaviours, such as being unable to stop yourself wanting to take things from shops without paying are connected with stress and depression, and where this appears to be the cause a counsellor might be able to help you decide what your next step might be.

Warning

Counsellors in the tradition we are talking about never agree to try to change people in order to suit other people. Indeed,

they do not set out to change people at all, though a large part
of their job is to enable people to make changes for themselves
which they really want to make.

A warning is in order though. The term 'counselling' is still
in use here and there to mean advice. Genetic counselling is
probably advice, to quote an innocent example. There are other
kinds of psuedo-counselling which are more sinister. Some
kinds of abortion counselling, for example, are probably
disguised forms of advice from people who cannot take a wholly
disinterested view of abortion. Also there are some so-called
counselling organisations which advise people not to continue
as practising homosexuals. The organisations we regard as
sinister in this respect try to change people to suit a particular
moral view of what people ought to be like, and have no
legitimate place in the therapy movement.

Uses of psychotherapy and analysis

Feeling stuck or lost
From time to time, most of us get a feeling of unhappiness
which is very distressing, but for which we are unable to find
an immediate cause. We might feel stuck or lost, or that we
have done a great many of the things in life we wanted to do
and have now apparently just run out of steam. This general
unease can be very difficult to talk about precisely because we
cannot separate it from life in general and label it as a problem
for which there might be an answer. It may be vaguely
connected with reaching a certain age – thirty or forty for
women, forty or fifty for men, for example – with a marriage
having lasted a certain number of years, with children having
grown up and no longer needing us to the same extent, or with
a reawakened grief from the past. Quite often we are not aware
even of a vague connection.

This kind of feeling, a signal to you that you are almost
certainly in need of some change of direction in your life, can
be very usefully taken for discussion with a counsellor.
However, it will be apparent from what we have said already
that something deeper and longer lasting would probably be of
more use than a short series of sessions or a one-off. It is, in
fact, not an uncommon reason for people to undertake
psychotherapy or to go into analysis.

Unconscious causes

What makes it a psychotherapy or analysis matter is the lack of clear and precise causes – they are there, obviously, but the client is not conscious of them. The objective of psychotherapy and analysis is often to enable the hidden, unconscious causes of unhappiness to be revealed, so that something more constructive or creative may be done in response to them.

So one of the things we can say about at least one sort of problem which is germane to these two kinds of therapy is that it often does not appear to be a problem as such, but nevertheless feels as though it is a problem. There need not be a crisis or emergency, and it may have no obvious connection with things like violence, grief, or family difficulties.

Looking deeper

The contract between the client or patient and the psychotherapist or analyst is comparatively long-term and provides for intensive work on both sides. So this kind of issue – vague unhappiness for no apparent reason – is only one of the reasons why people enter into such a contract. Any issue which a client feels he or she needs to explore in some depth is relevant. To illustrate the point, we can go back to the eight people who went to see the counsellor, and ask what they would have taken into psychotherapy or analysis.

Ron: The incident Ron described in which his wife broke up the kitchen, cried at a neighbour's house, and refused to see him, can be looked at two ways. He might present this as something about which he is very concerned, as indeed any man would be, and approach the issue in terms of being a good and patient husband who should do all he can to help his wife feel better. This seems on the face of it to be a reasonable and even generous response, considering what she did.

But another way of looking at it is to ask why he wants to be seen as patient, generous, reasonable, and managing. This position says a lot about him, and one of the things it says is that he is probably not facing up to his own inner needs. He may not recognise that such things do not happen in a vacuum, and that this must be an over-simplification of the incident. His wife is trying to tell him something. Can he listen?

The more we consider Ron himself, the move obvious it seems that he can benefit a great deal from looking deeply at his own life, to see how he came to be in this position, to see what he is getting out of it, and to decide for himself whether this is what he really wants. While he is doing this he will hopefully begin to see much more clearly what else he can do in future.

It seems likely that Mrs Ron would benefit from doing the same for herself, too. All this is likely to take quite a long time, and while counselling will help, a psychotherapy contract or long-term marriage counselling using some psychotherapy methods would offer each of them a better chance of success.

Dave: Dave, you will recall, has a mother who has stopped speaking to him because she disapproves of some aspect of his love life, and a father who usually says nothing but has now told Dave to leave home. His immediate issue is the need to find somewhere else to live. What might he take into psychotherapy or analysis?

As far as psychotherapy is concerned, this will depend on how distressed Dave is about the way his parents treat him, and whether or not he wants to tackle this. There will not be a lot of point in him going to see a therapist on a regular basis for a year or two if what he really wants to do is leave home and get on with his life. Immediate counselling is more likely to be of use to him. But if he can't leave home because he's the kind of person he is – and this must also be connected with the way his parents communicate with him – then psychotherapy would probably be a good place to start putting things right. As for analysis, this would almost certainly help him explore more deeply his relationships both with his parents and with the partner of whom his mother disapproves. He does not need any 'problem' at all to gain from it. However, given his age and life-style it seems unlikely that he would wish to make such a heavy commitment.

Mary: Dave does not seem trapped in any way, but Mary certainly is. Counselling will help her find the resources to explore and perhaps put into practice some new practical alternatives to wearing herself out visiting mother and feeling guilty, or banging her head against a brick wall trying to get her husband to help. Psychotherapy would help her get to the roots of her need to live this way – her need, in effect, to be trapped the way she is.

At the same time, it will also stir up things she may not be ready to face – her apparent need to put herself last not only in her relationship with her mother but also in the relationship with her husband will inevitably come under scrutiny. She will almost certainly question much more seriously and confidently whether she wants either relationship to go on in this way. A whole can of worms may have its lid removed, since she cannot become more self-determining without reviewing whether she wants to stay married and re-assessing what it is costing her to go on being a 'good daughter' for the rest of her mother's life. These are not easy issues for her to decide.

Jana: Can Jana escape the trap of her parents' expectations, and distance herself from them by her own efforts? This would be a very likely focus of her work with the counsellor, and could be done in more depth in psychotherapy. However, she is still at school, still very much under the direct control of her parents, and it seems likely that a full psychotherapy contract would not be feasible without their fully informed consent. However, this is one of the over-lap situations where a good counsellor would probably offer something very like psychotherapy to Jana so that she could gain the maximum benefit without feeling pressured into telling her parents.

George: Counselling would be used here to help George check out the serious aspects of his drinking problem, and may lead to him being given information about specialist agencies which could help him. If psychotherapy is to be a next step, then this will be because he and the therapist can usefully trace the causes of the drinking and because the therapist thinks George can probably gain enough insight into himself to find new ways of enjoying life. Analysis and psychotherapy are unlikely to be seen as an answer to the drinking itself, but might help him with the unhappiness which causes it.

George helps to illustrate the need for careful assessment before psychotherapy is undertaken.

Cynthia:There are many issues here which she could take into psychotherapy, particularly the connections which must exist between how she herself was treated as a child and the rift that apparently exists between her and her daughter. She is another example of somebody who, like Mary, would begin to think again about her marriage if she went into therapy.

Greg: Greg dresses up in his mother's clothes, and while being anxious about this behaviour, he is not very badly distressed. In counselling he may assess again his feelings about his parents, and any need he has for reassurance about his value in the family. The purely sexual connotations of his actions might well come last, since his starting point seems to be his relationship with his parents – for example, he began this when they were away, and continues it while they are out of the house on Saturdays. He may be looking for some reassurance about his normality. He could work on these issues almost equally well in counselling or in psychotherapy. The decision will probably turn on the extent of the commitment he is able to make.

Frank: He looks like somebody who will want counselling rather than psychotherapy. He has a clear objective – re-marriage – and has been thwarted in going ahead only by the dubious intervention of a friend. It may mean he wishes to reconsider the prospect of marriage generally, and counselling should help him decide whether this is so, and then enable him to do it if this is what he wants. Either way, he seems to be somebody who thinks that marrying again will solve all his problems, and this probably indicates that he lacks the insight to make good use of psychotherapy. This could easily be checked out in counselling. As far as analysis is concerned, his age may also be against him, and he is unlikely to be taken on.

Key points

It is fairly unlikely that every counsellor, psychotherapist, or analyst will agree with the points we have made in this chapter. We hope, however, that most of them will. The key points to remember are that almost every kind of problem is a good starting-point for counselling, and the only likely exceptions are addictions, and compulsive behaviour which require a specialist – but even then it is very unlikely indeed that you would be turned away unheard or even asked to leave as soon as your specialist needs become apparent. Counselling is the 'general practice' of the therapies, in other words.

There really aren't any problems which cannot be taken into psychotherapy either, but what makes it right or wrong for you is more to do with whether you want to go deeper into causes and have the time (and money) for this, or not. However, you can probably see much more clearly now, that psychotherapy and analysis are not basically to do with finding solutions to specific presenting problems. They could help a great many of the people who want to solve problems, and help them at a deeper level than counselling. This could stir up difficulties in relationships which are less than perfect, but which might be stable and useful, and it isn't always easy to weigh up the short-term aggravation against the longer-term chances of greater fulfilment. So some therapists use hybrid forms – Jana was an example of this – and many of the reputable psychotherapy associations expect you to have one or two preliminary sessions with an 'assessment therapist' before committing your time and money to a long-term contract, so you can take your time weighing up the risks.

Artificial distinction

Nevertheless, this is not the whole story. At the end of the day, this distinction between counselling and the other two therapies is almost certainly an artificial one. Good therapists offer the client the same kind of relationship, the same opportunity to explore connections, the same availability of a space where the client can be listened to and acknowledged and respected whether what is happening is called counselling, psychotherapy, or analysis. How far the client goes has to be a matter for the client.

Brian Thorne, whom we interviewed with his colleagues Prue Conradi and Faith Broadbent at the Norwich Centre, put it in a nutshell for us.

We believe quite explicity that the client knows best, in the sense that the client knows what he or she really wishes to do. Therefore, to have some kind of cut-off point in one's own mind is actually to diddle the client out of the fulfilment of those wishes. So if a client really only wants to explore, say, a passing situation or difficulty, and having explored that satisfactorily wishes to say goodbye – well, that is the client's choice, and that is right and proper. But if that same client comes for counselling feeling that is all he or she wants to do, but as the process develops, begins to move into much deeper water and wants to stay there or go further, then it will seem to me pretty catastrophic if the counsellor or therapist then says – I'm awfully sorry, we can't go there, and that's my cut-off point, and now you must go off and see a psychotherapist or an analyst. So we don't work in that kind of way.

PART III
METHODS OF THERAPY

8   A special relationship

The basic claim that is made for therapy – whether we call it counselling, psychotherapy, or analysis – is that it enables people to get more out of life by becoming psychologically healthier. Our next objective is to look at the methods which are used to achieve this.

In this chapter we concentrate on the relationship between the therapist and the client – what is known in the jargon as the 'therapeutic' or health-enhancing relationship. It is generally agreed that this is crucial to the whole process of therapy. What is it about it that does the trick?

The talking cure

The first point to note is that there would be no therapy at all, but for the very special relationship which is built up between the therapist and the client. The therapy *is* the relationship. After all, there are no artificial aids – no pills or potions, no crutches or scapels. An early patient of Freud called therapy 'the talking cure', and this is what it is. At the centre of therapy there are two people and a lot of talk. How they talk, what they talk about, and the way they treat one another is what constitutes the therapy.

This is no ordinary relationship, but a curious one in some respects, full of paradoxes. It is very intimate, in the sense that the topics it deals with are extremely personal – the closely guarded secrets of the client, his or her deepest and most significant experiences in life, the feelings the client has about himself or herself which are most protected and most often hidden from view. Yet it is still a professional relationship, with clear boundaries designed to prevent it ever becoming more than this or less than this.

It is also in some ways a risky relationship. Within it the

client takes the risk of letting out destructive and painful
feelings, feelings which would be hurtful in the extreme if they
were let out elsewhere. The client is allowed, in fact
encouraged to lose many inhibitions. Yet it is also a very safe
and secure relationship, often the most secure the client has
known as long as he or she can remember.

It is obvious, therefore, that a great deal of hard work has to
go into setting up and maintaining it – and, when the work is
done, into ending it. This work often begins with the formation
of some kind of contract between therapist and client.

The contract

The purpose of a contract is to give the relationship as much
security as possible. It helps the client to know where he or she
stands, and contributes to the development of trust. This is
especially important in counselling, because the client may
only be coming to one session, and there will be no time for a
gradual consolidation of trust over many weeks or months as
there will be in analysis or psychotherapy.

So counselling often begins with a brief explanation from the
counsellor as to how he or she wants to work. For example, the
counsellor will probably say how much time is available – it
might be 'as long as you need', or it might be one, two, or three
hours. (Three hours, by the way, is generally regarded as a
very long session, and open ended sessions are comparatively
rare.) Any necessary agreement about fees can also be reached
at this stage.

Then the ground rules might be spelled out – for example,
that the client can feel free to say anything or express any
feelings, however destructive or distressing, and that what is
said will be confidential between them. It might also be felt
necessary to add that the counsellor will spend most of the time
listening. At some point in all this, if there is a specific
objective which the client wishes to achieve, as sometimes
there is, then therapist and client agree how this shall be
defined. It may sound a lot to cover, but in fact all this is done
briefly, and in a manner which helps to build up trust.

In psychotherapy and analysis also, the contract is designed
to offer security to the client. The question of fees is settled in
much the same way, and specific objectives, where these apply,
are defined. Dates and times are agreed for sessions, and these
tend to be regularly spaced – the client comes to see the
therapist at the same hour on the same days of the week, each
time for fifty minutes – the therapist will almost always finish

on time. The rule about saying whatever you feel regardless of whether you think it will be absurd or destructive or shocking also applies – indeed, this is Freud's rule of 'free association'.

The fact that the sessions are regular means that the client and the therapist think of these times as belonging only to the client. Many therapists also believe that the regular time-frame has a security of its own, akin to the way children feel secure knowing that something they need will always be there for them. It also encourages the client to set aside time in advance for the therapy and to see this as work, with its own special time and place, like having a job to do. The work that is done with the therapist will largely be restricted to these times, although this does not mean that telephone contact between sessions is necessarily discouraged.

All this may be underlined by the fact that it is customary for sessions which are arranged but which the client does not attend to be charged for – though this practice is not universal, and some therapists prefer to offer a double session to make up for the loss.

Acquaintance

Before any close relationship can exist, the two people concerned have to get to know one another. In therapy this tends to happen at different speeds and reach different degrees of depth, according to how much time is available. In a one-off counselling session, for example, or as part of a short series of sessions, the acquaintance process has to be accelerated more than it would be in, say, three years of twice a week psychotherapy, or in five years of daily analysis. At the same time, of course, it is unlikely to reach quite the same depth in a one-off as it would in, say analysis.

The therapist who is working as a counsellor, therefore, tends to ask more questions. Some of these are necessary to elicit information about the client and his or her world. But they are not the kinds of question which an interviewer would ask, designed solely to obtain information for the use of the questioner. Most of them are open-ended – not easily answered by a simple yes or no. Most of them are also about feelings. In fact, counsellors, in common with all therapists, try to manage with as few questions as possible. They certainly do not quiz their clients. They try to get them talking freely and naturally and then listen intently and learn as much as they can from what they hear.

At the same time it is important to note that time spent on

acquaintance is nearly always used one-sidedly. That is to say, the therapist sets out to get to know the client, but does not spend an equal amount of time talking about himself or herself as would happen in the building up of an ordinary relationship. Of course this is partly because the session is primarily to meet the client's needs, not those of the therapist. But it also helps to keep the relationship on a professional footing – the two of them are not there for a cosy chat or to get to know one another as if they were at a party or meeting on a train. For the same reason socialising between sessions is discouraged.

In some traditions of therapy – notably the psycho-dynamic one – therapists are also concerned for technical reasons to give out very little private information about themselves. They believe that clients quite naturally fill the gap this leaves by imagining things about their therapist. Too much actual information would restrict this process, and they argue that what we imagine can be extremely useful as a way into a deeper understanding of our unconscious needs and fantasies.

Quality of the relationship

Setting up clear contracts to provide security, building up trust, and keeping things on a professional footing are obviously important. But what makes therapy possible is something which has much more to do with the quality of the relationship than with the arrangements the two people make about the work. From start to finish, the therapy relationship depends for its effectiveness on each client being met as a unique individual.

Of course, the same kind of thing could be said about many relationships. The difference here is that the therapy relationship sets out to achieve this from the start, and has no other objective than this. So it is not simply something which can be observed in a detached kind of way as a general truism or a cliché – it is felt deeply by both parties to be the central truth of their own particular relationship. They become close not out of the sheer accident of chemistry – though this undoubtedly helps the relationship along where it happens – but because the therapist invests great skill and energy in making it happen. He or she is there for the client, not there for anybody else or for any other reason.

Each moment of the therapist's contribution to the relationship emphasises this fact. We said just now that each client is *met* as a unique individual. That does not mean met at

the door, or met now and then, but met every moment of each
session.

All this means, of course, that the client is treated as a very
special person. At the same time, this is done not by using a
good bedside manner, or by the careful application of shrewdly
calculated expertise – though it has to be said that neither of
these is necessarily a bad thing. Whatever happens is that the
therapist believes in the fact that each client is unique. The
healing nature of the relationship – the element within it
which makes people feel capable of enhancing their own value
to themselves – is intimately connected with the transmission
of this belief as the constant response by the therapist to
whatever the client does.

If for a moment we stand back from this and think about it, we
surely cannot help but be struck by how rarely such a
relationship occurs in our every day lives. It has some of the
qualities of care and love about it which we associate with
parenting, especially the moments of complete acceptance which
occur when mother and infant form their closest ties, or the
moments of complete fellowship when we merge into a group of
companions with complete mutual acceptance and a completely
unselfconscious sense of belonging. At the same time there is
enough space in the relationship for the client to choose the
distance with which he or she is comfortable, and enough
flexibility to be angry knowing that this will not lead to rejection.

Tailor-made therapy

This central fact of therapy – that each client is met as a
unique individual – helps to explain some of the difficulty all
commentators have in describing what happens in therapy
sessions. For one thing, it means that each client–therapist
relationship is unique, and therefore therapy itself is that
much harder to generalise about. Also, there simply cannot be
a set procedure for therapy. The therapist cannot hold this
belief and put it into practice if he or she sets out by applying a
formula, even one which is fairly loose and can be adapted to
take account of individual variations from the average.

So what actually happens in therapy is composed on the spot.
Counselling, psychotherapy and analysis are careful and
sensitive procedures which have to be made up for us as we go
along. The therapist cannot know, except perhaps in the very
broadest terms, what will happen in a session. It has to be
discovered, and the response to it invented at the moment of
discovery.

This is not to say that therapists do not know what they are doing, but rather to say that they are there to respond to what we are doing, and they cannot know what this will be until we do it. Each session has to be bespoke; there can be no such thing as off-the-peg therapy. This is why everybody's experience of therapy is different from everybody else's.

Rejecting the relationship

Of course, being treated as a complete, acceptable, unique individual by the therapist may sound to some people like a version of paradise on earth – something they may feel is to be basked in and enjoyed. It isn't hard to imagine them grinning, and rubbing their hands, and saying, 'Marvellous – I could do with a basinful of that, lying there and enjoying all that attention. Lead me to it!'

But this takes little account of the realities of the world we live in, the world we grow up in. In fact it is not an easy relationship for most of us to accept. We are used to being treated very differently from this. We are quite likely to be suspicious of it, to reject this view of ourselves. There are lamentably few of us who can claim in all honesty that we really accept our own uniqueness, really accept and love ourselves unreservedly. Instead we constantly question our own value, whilst craving for others to accept it. The contradiction between the way the therapist treats us and the way we treat ourselves throws into stark and painful relief the truth about us – that we have learned the hard way to belittle ourselves, and that the pain of these lessons is still there, not far beneath the surface of our pretended autonomy and confidence.

So therapy frequently consists of a battle between these two opposing views of us, a battle which goes on inside us, which has probably raged for most of our life, but which now comes into the open. The part of us which wants to be accepted and loved for its own sake battles with the bit of us which is certain we do not qualify for this.

If what we are setting out to do is find the answer to particular problems, then we shall probably not wish to understand how the battle began. We shall not wish to trace this conflict back to its roots. It will be enough, so to speak, to win a skirmish or two – to feel acceptable enough, good enough for now to regain some of our confidence and face the future with a bit more hope.

If we are seeking a major change in the direction or purpose of our life, we may want to understand much more. We shall want to know how this conflict began, why we still cannot accept ourselves as good enough, and what we can do to become acceptable to ourselves.

A laboratory experiment

The truth about therapy, then, is that learning about ourselves would be impossible without that very special relationship and the quality that makes it special. But we do not learn easily, or painlessly. Nevertheless, we can learn. As we test the acceptability of the therapist's belief in us we begin to test-drive new ways of relating.

In short-term therapy, the new perspective which we gain from being accepted and listened to and valued for ourselves helps us to see that we have more options than we realised. We can discuss new ways of tackling the difficult parts of our life, trying them out for size. The people who would be threatened by this are not there to be hurt or frightened by our thoughts, so we can explore these thoughts openly. Feeling valued helps us by giving us the confidence to use therapy as a laboratory where we can experiment with feeling better, and begin to get used to the idea.

In a long-term therapy relationship we have more time to try out many more ways of being who we are, ways which we used at different stages of childhood, ways we learned in adolescence, ways we have just invented. It becomes not only a unique experience, as we have seen, but also a highly creative one. At its best it enables us to design new behaviours for ourselves and try them out in the space that becomes available due to the skill of the therapist.

9 Skills of the therapist

Maintaining any kind of relationship can take a lot of hard work and skill, and the therapeutic relationship is hardly likely to be an exception, particularly when we consider how unusual it is. The next step, therefore, is to look at some of the key technical skills of the therapist.

The two we are going to concentrate on have technical names – one is called 'working with transference', and the other is called 'interpretation'. You have, of course, heard of them already – Derek Blows referred to them when he was talking about the differences between counselling and the longer-term therapies. But before we go on to describe them so you will know rather more about what to expect if you go into therapy, we have to say a little bit about why they are important to therapy generally.

Background

Most of the different varieties of counselling, psychotherapy and analysis belong to the same family of health-enhancing activities in the sense that they all have the same grandfather – Sigmund Freud, born 1856 in Moravia, who lived his most significant years in Vienna, and died in London in 1939. The two techniques which we are going to look at are most commonly associated with the kind of therapy he developed, known today as psycho-dynamic therapy. Indeed, 'transference' and 'interpretation' are translations of his words, and refer basically to ideas which he used in order to explain and understand what happens in therapy. We shall not need to go very deeply into explaining these ideas – all that will be necessary is to say how they are used and what this will mean to you as a client. But we do need to put the ideas into perspective before we start, because there is quite a lot of disagreement about them amongst therapists.

What has happened is that like any interesting family,

therapy has moved on since Freud's day. His ideas have been safe-guarded and nurtured by one branch of the family, but challenged and developed, and in some cases more or less completely rejected by other branches. So there are counsellors, psychotherapists, and analysts today who use transference and make interpretations in much the same way as he did, some who prefer to do these things a different way, and some who say they do not do them at all. Nevertheless, these two techniques are so important that every therapist without exception has views on them.

There is every likelihood that if you decide to undertake either short-term or long-term therapy, your therapist will use some version of these skills. Even more importantly, if for any reason you feel uncomfortable with a therapist, it is likely to be because of the way he or she works, or does not work with transference, or because of the use he or she makes or does not make of interpretation. So you need to understand them not just out of interest, or to get a better idea of what therapy is like, but also to help you decide what might be going wrong if ever therapy seems not to be working for you.

Transference

Transference is something which happens between the person who is receiving analysis or psychotherapy or counselling, and the person who is giving it. In effect it is the way the patient or client begins to respond to the therapist by 'transferring' feelings to him or her which once belonged more importantly to somebody else – usually somebody significant in the early life of the patient or client, such as a parent or grandparent, uncle, or brother or sister.

When you think about it, it is fairly obvious that something like this is more or less inevitable in any close relationship. If anybody you meet starts to become important to you, he or she begins to fill some of the gaps in your life left by the people whom you were once close to but who are not there any more or who seem to have changed. The more you rely on the friend to understand you, the more this is likely to happen. Perhaps consciously, and certainly unconsciously, you start to treat such people as if they were these earlier people – because this will mean that they are more likely to treat you the way the earlier people did.

Of course, this can happen with good feelings or with bad ones. For example, you might have had a favourite grandfather whom you loved dearly and could get round very easily by making your eyes bigger and wheedling a little bit. When you feel warm towards somebody who is good to you in the same kind of way, you might start producing exactly this response, sometimes without being aware that this is what you are doing, and at other times, only just conscious that thoughts of your grandfather have come into your head. But equally, if you hated your grandfather for some reason, and were scared of him, then there will be times when what gets transferred into a present relationship are these feelings of fear and rejection. You will probably be unaware of why you react this way at the time, and may even pooh-pooh the notion that there is a connection, but a therapist who understands transference would not be so likely to do so.

Using transference

We saw earlier that some therapists deliberately say very little about themselves because clients quite naturally start to fill the gaps in for themselves. This encourages transference, and helps the therapy along. By working to provide a framework which accepts transference when it happens, and by being aware of it when it does happen, the therapist can get a really valuable insight into early relationships and experiences that still hurt.

But that isn't all. Once the therapist knows that a particular set of feelings is being transferred from you, he or she can take the necessary steps to enable you to see this for yourself. This gives the therapist an opportunity to help you remember more about what happened – the incidents that led up to you feeling the way you do. Quite often also, once you have remembered you can start to understand these past events in a different light.

Therapists who work with this idea also study their own responses to the client, because sometimes you may trigger off a response in them which may or may not belong to the therapy itself. For example, the therapist might get a feeling of being shut out by you. This feeling might belong to the therapist's past – and be unrelated to the therapy – or may be a feeling evoked by how you were once made to feel. This is known as 'counter-transference'.

Going wrong

You can probably see now why it is so useful to understand this aspect of therapy. For one thing, it means that clients often have very strong feelings about their therapists – feelings which belong in part to the reality of the relationship, but also feelings which are hard to explain without some recognition of the idea of transference. Suppose, then, that you start therapy, and find quite quickly that you have become very emotionally attached to the therapist. Or suppose that the reverse happens, and that you feel extremely angry with him or her. These things are not as fanciful as they might seem – they can happen quite easily in counselling and psychotherapy, and are widely believed to be the norm at some stage during analysis. The problem is that you may be unable to sort out whether these feelings belong to the reality of the relationship or are directly caused by transference.

This can make the feelings very much worse, too, because of all the confusion and the difficulty of explaining to other people how you really feel. But what can make a difficult situation into one which is almost impossible is when your therapist does not understand the dangers of mixing up his or her private life with your therapy. Professional boundaries are there to prevent this sort of thing happening, and both the training of the therapist and the conditions under which he or she works should also guard against such accidents.

The best way to avoid this risk is to choose a therapist who is properly trained, aware of the dangers, and has what is called a 'supervisor' – another therapist to whom he or she reports regularly on a professional basis to discuss the progress of his or her work. If this proves not to be enough, then in the first place the feelings should be discussed in therapy, and if necessary discussed with another therapist from a reputable organisation.

It is also very important for us to emphasise that the risk of therapy going wrong is not all that great, and that whether or not your therapist belongs to the Freudian tradition makes very little difference to this risk. All professional, properly trained therapists know about it and will be very careful about transference.

The art of interpretation

The simplest way to explain about interpretation is probably to go back to the early days of psycho-analysis when Freud was struggling to understand the very distressed people who came to him for help. He came to believe that behind the apparent lack of logic in the way unhappy, distressed people behave lay a very special, personal logic, almost like another language system. The role of the therapist was to act as a kind of interpreter – to listen very carefully and figure out what this behaviour was saying about the feelings locked up inside them.

He became convinced that we all have an unconscious mental life which explains why so many of us have strange rituals when under stress, why we have puzzling dreams, why we sometimes make accidental slips of the tongue which give away secret wishes, why we have characteristic mannerisms. He also recognised how distressing it can be when we do such irrational things, know we are doing them, maybe wish we didn't do them, but cannot see why we do them. So he began to help his patients in effect to read the code-words of their own behaviour, so they could become fully aware of what was going on inside them. He became convinced that when people really know the origins of their unwanted bits of behaviour they can manage without them.

This view is widely accepted today, particularly amongst counsellors and psychotherapists trained in the tradition started by Freud. The basic idea is that very little that is distressing happens to you purely by accident – there is an unconscious cause somewhere at the back of all of it. By using the interpretations of the therapist to guide us, we can discover what causes our pain and distress and make new choices as to what we do about it. Today many therapists use some form of interpretation, though they may not call it this.

Interpretation, then, is the art of selecting some of these clues to what may be going on inside you, and putting them to you to see whether this helps you understand yourself. It is an art far more than it is a science – the therapist uses the technique creatively to help you, not scientifically to analyse you relentlessly, to discover the truth regardless of what happens or how you feel. So not everything that he or she sees in what you do will be interpreted.

There is also an art in the way you are given interpretations, that is to say, the way they are said. In most types of therapy the therapist is unlikely to say – 'Now, look here, what you are really saying is . . .' She or he is much more likely to offer interpretation in a very tentative way, giving you the choice of looking into yourself to see if this feels right. When it works, this method can produce amazing insights into things which had puzzled you for a very long time. When it doesn't work, the fact that it was so tentative usually means you simply reject it casually and carry on without noticing.

We said 'most types of therapy' – but of course, there are exceptions. Some therapists deliver their interpretations forcefully, some do it in a detached and clinical way, and some do it almost all the time whilst yet others do it very sparingly.

Helpful interpretation

Perhaps the most important aspect of the art of giving interpretation is that it is done to help you, the client, not to prove how clever the therapist is. What is said will help you best if it meets certain criteria, and, indeed, you can begin to assume that there is something wrong about the therapy if interpretations do not meet them except on rare occasions. Again, if this happens, discuss it with the therapist first, and if necessary seek a second opinion.

There are three main criteria. First, it should stimulate insight. A good interpretation tells you something about yourself which you can recognise and accept as true, but have not recognised before in quite the same way. Secondly, it should fit readily into the category of questions which you are asking yourself at the time. An interpretation may be valid and useful, but if you have to interrupt your current thoughts and change the subject you will probably resent this and reject the truth of what is said by the therapist. Interpretation should not result in the therapist taking over the work, but should be an aid to you doing the work. Thirdly, it should simplify, not complicate the issues. Of course, this may not be immediately apparent to you. You may have to accept certain thoughts and feelings about yourself which are uncomfortable, and which you might prefer to reject at the time that the interpretation is given. But if you are able to accept these aspects of yourself the interpretation will make sense and simplify things for you.

For example, suppose you are in a psychotherapy session, and you are 'thinking aloud'. You have been talking about your feelings concerning a brother who seemed to get better treatment from your parents then you did. The therapist is listening very closely, and when you pause and go into quite a deep feeling, she says: 'Maybe you felt very envious of your brother.'

This sentence is the therapist's interpretation of your behaviour at that moment. At once you reply: 'Oh no – I never ever felt jealous of him. He deserved everything he got.'

Consider these words for a moment, as a therapist might do. First, the instant denial, even as you produce it, seems to escape from you too quickly as though you were responding to an accusation, not just a neutral comment. Next, it comes out as a sweeping statement – 'never' – and it is surely unlikely that the truth could be quite so absolute as this. Also, you took the word 'envious' and turned it into the word 'jealous'. Finally, there is the double meaning in the last sentence. It might mean that he merited the better treatment he received, or it might mean that something bad happened to him and he deserved this. 'He deserved everything he got' is something we often say when we feel that a person has been justly punished. The therapist is quite likely to take this to mean that she was correct in her interpretation. What has probably happened is that you have often felt envious, but for a very long time have not felt safe to express this feeling because you were afraid of being accused of jealousy. She will probably not say anything, though, just wait in silence, perfectly relaxed, giving you the space to feel whatever feelings come to you.

All being well, the interpretation from the therapist will stay in your mind and enable you to question why you are denying your own inner feelings. If so it might lead you to a new insight – such as remembering a forgotten incident in which you were slapped by your parents for 'being jealous' – and help you along in your own train of thought. If it does not do any of these things because you really were never envious or jealous, or because you were, but still cannot recognise this fact, then the therapist's interpretation will feel unimportant to you, and hardly interrupt what you are doing. Her silence will simply enable you to move on.

Feelings about the therapist

In psychotherapy, particularly those varieties which are in the post-Freudian, or psycho-dynamic tradition, it is not uncommon for quite a lot of the interpretation to concentrate on the feelings the client or patient has towards the therapist. This is because it is being used within the transference which we talked about earlier in this chapter.

A common example of this has to do with those occasions when the therapist goes away on holiday – incidentally, one of the things we discovered in our research was that just like the Republic of France, psychotherapists and analysts tend to go away on holiday for the whole of the month of August. Before the annual break, or when there are other holiday breaks, therapists expect their clients to react with conscious or unconscious distress to the separation, to get a little bit more withdrawn, or crotchety, or become more effusive in their praise of the therapist.

The idea behind this common expectation is that when we

start to trust people and rely on them being there for us we feel resentment when they go away. By discussing this the therapist can test out the extent of the trust that has developed. Also, the way that such signs of unconscious distress are revealed will speak volumes about early experiences of being left without support, and can be used to help the client understand what he or she went through at the time, and then relate it to his or her present-day concerns.

Who is in control?

Another very common area on which interpretation concentrates in psychotherapy is control – who is in charge of the session? When you and I become clients we are very clever at keeping control. In everyday life everybody manages the information he or she presents to others about himself or herself. We choose what to wear depending on how we want to be seen, we design our faces with make-up or without it, with beards or moustaches or without them, and we choose our particular hairstyles, all so that we can have a degree of control over the way other people will treat us or not treat us. On top of this, we design for ourselves a unique and characteristic set of non-verbal communication methods, a whole personal dialect of body language so that people will know who we are and what we do and what to expect from us, and how to treat us or how not to treat us. These things show in the way we walk, sit, stand, speak, move, smile, touch, accept or reject different amounts of closeness, and so on.

These ways we have of presenting ourselves amount to a set of controls, applied inwards as self-control, and outwards as other-control. We are often so used to them that we are quite unaware what we are saying about ourselves every moment of the day and night. Most of us are much more controlled and controlling than we realise. Furthermore, at those times in our lives when we are up against it, we become more controlling of ourselves or others – in just the same way that any system which is threatened will try to tighten up its procedures to lower the risk of nasty things happening. Indeed, evidence of tight control is usually taken as evidence of great hurt. If we are not hurt or afraid of being hurt, then we can generally get by with less control.

In order to enable a client to become more himself or herself the psychotherapist has to get inside the perimeter of these controls, to be admitted to the presence of the real person inside, rather than to the controlled person who is so often being presented. Unless this happens the client will be there physically, but not fully there in the psychological sense. So the therapist who senses that controls are being used in the session to keep him or her out will often use interpretation in an attempt to get the client to be less controlling. For example, the client who says nothing for a long time may be told something like: 'I feel that you are keeping me out,' or 'It seems that you have feelings you wish to keep from me.' Of course, such things will only be said if the therapist believes that this is the case. Control is quite likely to be an issue in the early stages of all therapy, but it will obviously come up in a very individual way.

10 Stages of therapy

Going into therapy, then, means taking part in a process which is going to change you in some significant way if it is to be at all worthwhile. Going into counselling does not mean this to quite the same extent, but because of the overlap between the two it often does mean something of the sort. The process, as we have seen, does not work the same way for everybody, so it is hard to generalise about it.

Nevertheless, it will be clear from what has been said so far that if you work regularly with a therapist either for counselling or psychotherapy or analysis there are going to be several different phases in the process. The next step is to look at these, and some of the challenges they may face you with not only inside, but also outside therapy. We shall do this with particular reference to medium-and long-term therapy relationships.

Acquaintance stage

At the start your therapist does not know you, but will need to get to know you. So this phase, when the primary result of the sessions for the therapist is that he or she has an increased acquaintance of you, is one where a great deal of learning goes on for both participants. We could quite accurately call it the 'acquaintance stage'.

There may not, however, be nearly so much consciousness of change at this stage. Both of you are testing one another out – deciding deep matters about trusting and caring, about dependence and control. The therapist needs to gain an insight into how you work – the kinds of self-insights that are already there, the kinds that are not, and those which will be easy or difficult to build as the sessions proceed. The important thing to remember is that you can be yourself quite safely. You do not have to be consistent in everything you say, nor create a good impression. But you are likely to find this hard work.

Some therapists may ask you to consider using the couch, and however nicely this is put, you know you are expected to agree to this. He or she will probably explain that this is likely to make you feel very exposed at first, perhaps quite helpless, and that for some reason feelings can seem very much more vivid than if you sit in a chair and face the therapist. Using the couch the first few times will take courage on your part. You may need to be a little kinder to yourself for the rest of the day. But even if you use the couch, you should not be forced to go on using it if you do not wish to.

You will probably have a lot on your plate outside the sessions at this stage. For many of us there is the problem of persuading others to feel good about the therapy. There may be husbands, wives, lovers, friends, colleagues, parents and children in your life who have resisted the idea, actively or passively, and who will need time to accept it, or who will not fully accept it. Most of us who go for help want those close to us to understand our decision and to support us in it, even though we ourselves may not be entirely clear why we have taken this step. It is not uncommon to feel any gap that existed before growing wider.

This is not helped in the early days of therapy by the fact that it is very hard to explain what exactly we do. Indeed, we may not exactly 'do' anything, or at least not anything others are willing to recongise as a 'real' or 'valuable' activity. Just being yourself in the presence of somebody who accepts you is an alien experience to many strong and powerful people. Their lives are expressed only through the energetic and competitive pursuit of tangible objectives. If they do not understand how to just 'be there' themselves, it will be hard for them to understand how you can do it. They may not make much of an effort to try to understand.

These perceptions can very usefully be talked about in the sessions. Your relationships are a fundamental part of you, and anything which happens outside sessions can be a good starting point for therapy.

Crying

We also have to bear in mind that people who go into therapy because they are hurt or angry do so as hurt and angry people. Tears are shed in the session and outside it often far more readily than at any other time in the person's life. There is no rule that you have to cry, but you probably will.

Therapy also stirs up painful memories, which can leave you feeling raw and vulnerable. This can be really bewildering during the first stage, because you will not have begun yet to fit the work into the sessions. It tends to spill out into the time between sessions. Controlling this is hard work, and if you feel very tired around the time of your sessions this can be the explanation.

Clients often think of their therapy during this stage as something they are trying out, not necessarily something they are fully committed to. They see themselves as people who are taking their problems to the helper, rather than people who are taking themselves there, and the extent of their commitment will depend on how they feel about the problems, not how they feel about themselves. There is a strangeness about it too. They are not used to it. You may need to allow for the fact that there is a great deal to learn, not just about yourself and the therapist, but also about people around you, and about the sheer mechanics of fitting the sessions into your life.

Trusting stage

All this means that the first phase cannot start to give way to a different set of feelings until the client relaxes into an acceptance of the habit of therapy. The regular sessions – same time, same place, each week – which occur in psychotherapy begin to provide a new sense of security. Going to the sessions starts to become more familiar, more of a habit. You get used to the journey, to the timing, to the room where the therapy takes place.

The second phase is reached when you have stopped questioning whether to trust the therapist and yourself, and when you begin to accept the general value of your therapy. You begin to attend as yourself, to feel that whatever anybody else may say or think it is worth going for its own sake. It would be appropriate to call this the 'trusting stage'.

This is the point at which transference is clearly established. Now the relationship between you and the therapist becomes a kind of arena in which piece by piece your life-play is acted out and interpreted. There is a lot to get through. No part of your experience can be written off as irrelevant. All of it may need to come under scrutiny.

Sometimes this is done entirely through the expression of feelings, sometimes by means of factual or rational discussion, and often through a mixture of both. Within the psycho-dynamic tradition of therapy the subject matter of many sessions is likely to be your early experience – memories of childhood are opened up so that long-forgotten feelings can be looked at again and then re-lived as if they were happening today, and little by little you come to understand them more fully. The understanding that results is a complex mixture of feelings and thoughts, and sometimes things which make sense as feelings make little or no sense as thoughts.

At other times the reverse of this happens. But there are also times when thought and feeling come together to make sense in a wholly new way – a kind of 'think–feel' way.

Trust between therapist and client enables discoveries to be made. Many of these are about the way that early experience still affects us. We begin to see that things we do today began with events in childhood, and that we are still reacting to today's events using the repertoire of childhood. Recognising how inappropriate this is helps to free us from the emotional necessity of behaving this way, and we can choose more appropriate responses as a result.

It is not uncommon during the 'trusting phase' for the therapy sessions to become the most significant events of your week. Other concerns may be forgotten or neglected. The person you are in therapy can become more important to you than who you are thought to be outside it.

There may be times, even if you have established a trust in your therapist, when you feel very angry, or threatened, or misunderstood. If your therapy is good enough these feelings can be explored and worked through.

You may begin to see that you are trying outside therapy to change more radically into the person you are inside it. You experiment with change in the sessions, establish that you can do it, and gain the confidence to try it outside.

Separation phase

The third and final phase probably begins with a growing awareness that you have already started to separate from the therapist, that you have taken over the role for yourself and now mange your life as if you were your own therapist. This is the 'separation phase', when you begin to feel that the chapter in your life when you needed to go back and look again at how you became who you are is drawing to its close.

Everything you have done in therapy up to this point – the learning how to trust, the changes you have tested and then tried for yourself – takes on a new perspective. It begins to feel as though it belongs to the past, rather than to the present. You are ready to take charge of your own future in a lighter, easier way than would have felt possible when therapy began. It may also be a time of sadness – a time to mourn an important relationship that will, by its very nature, have to come to an end. The two of you negotiate the close of the therapy. You once spent many hours learning to be a client, and now you learn to be not a client.

PART IV
CHOICE OF THERAPY

11 Choosing a Therapist

Therapy is not an easy option. For it to be of any use you have to stick at it and work hard on yourself, facing up to your need to change, re-experiencing bits of the past which still hurt, maybe keeping yourself going in spite of the opposition or ignorance of people close to you. It requires courage on your part, skill and encouragement from your therapist.

Without the right therapist, it is an even harder option. How do you find this person? How can you give yourself the best chance from the start of getting the therapist you need? What choices are there? These are the issues to which we turn next.

Emergency or not?

How you set about choosing somebody for yourself depends in the first place on two factors – how urgent this is, and where you live. In an emergency of any sort you probably feel first of all that you need practical help. If you can get this kind of help locally, from the doctor, through an organisation, a neighbour, a member of your family, or a friend, then obviously you should do so, just so that you can cope with the immediate issues. The essential point to remember, however, is that once you have secured your ability to cope in the short-term, you will need to start straight away making some better arrangement. This is where counselling comes in.

The people who will know about your local counselling services are voluntary organisations such as the citizens advice bureau, local churches, and neighbourhood associations. The public library is an excellent place to ask, and most town halls have an information officer who will have a list of voluntary organisations. If you are absolutely stuck, try contacting the nearest Samaritans branch – their telephone number will be in your directory under 'S'. Samaritans are not counsellors, and they take great pride in this fact, since it has helped them be of use over the years to many suicidal people who would have been put off by talking to some kind of expert, rather than to somebody like themselves. But they quite often know where the trained counsellors are in their locality.

The British Association for Counselling can be phoned at their national office, listed on page 109, and so can several other national bodies. Contacting a counsellor or therapist this way can be rather slow.

Take your time

Emergencies apart, how do you find a therapist? Again it partly depends on where you live. Therapists are not distributed evenly around the country. Most of them are to be found in London and the counties nearby, and although parts of the north-west, and the larger cities in Scotland, Wales, and the north-east are fairly well served, there are still vast areas of Britain where prospective clients will find there is very little choice, and the nearest therapist is too far away for easy access.

Your local Yellow Pages might be useful, and another very good way is by the personal recommendation of somebody you know who has worked with a particular therapist. But be careful! At present there is no law to prevent anyone setting up as a 'counsellor', 'therapist', 'analyst', unlike doctors who must register before they can practise. Moves are afoot within the profession to change this, but at the time of writing, no national register of therapists exists.

On the whole it is best to find a therapist through one of the national organisations. Use the resource section on pages 109–13 or your local information services to find out names and addresses of organisations, and then telephone or write to them. Since you will probably want to make a considered judgement, what we need to do next is look at some of the things you might take into account. This is a little more complicated than it might seem at first sight.

Bona fides

Therapists, as we have spoken of them so far, are fully qualified professionals. That means three things.

First, it means that they have completed some kind of

training course or have been accredited in some way by a reputable national organisation. Secondly, it means that they are aware of the risks of what they do – to their clients and to themselves – and have taken the necessary steps accepted in their profession to minimise these risks. In the context of therapy this means essentially that they have what is called a 'supervisor', somebody they see on a regular professional basis themselves with whom they discuss issues arising in counselling so they are still learning, and so their own lives do not become entangled with their clients' lives at a personal level. The supervisor should be an experienced professional therapist.

Thirdly, a fully qualified professional therapist will be a member of the community of therapists. That is to say he or she will not be a loner, practising without reference to what is going on in the world of therapy, but a member of some kind of organisation or network which is accountable publicly, which has a code of conduct, and which can seriously discipline those of its members who are guilty of misconduct by expelling them.

You have a right to ask anybody whom you might go to see for therapy about his or her training, supervision, and membership of organisations, and you would be well advised to exercise this right. It is all too easy to assume that the person is formally qualified, and to find out later that this is not the case. If you feel a bit nervous about asking, try raising it at the very first session, or telephone or write immediately after the first session.

Training

This is almost certainly the most important of the three issues. The therapy movement has grown haphazardly and rapidly over the last few years, and one of the things which has improved immensely is the training of therapists. What kind of training should you look for in a therapist?

Counsellors

The training of counsellors has not been nearly so rigorous as that of psychotherapists until quite recently, and it is still very patchy. Most of the leading organisations now believe that a minimum training should consist of either a one-year full-time course, or a three-year part-time course. If a person calls himself or herself a counsellor, and is doing so on the basis of training lasting less than thirty hours in total, then you should be extremely suspicious.

For example, there are now literally hundreds of organisations in the management training business which run courses on counselling skills for managers. Reputable ones will emphasise to the trainees that their course does not qualify people as counsellors, merely introduce them to the basics of counselling skills. The less reputable ones do not do this, and in any case there is nothing to stop somebody saying he or she is a trained counsellor regardless. Some training in counselling skills is also included on the curriculum for certain kinds of nurse. This is not enough by itself to make them into professional counsellors. Nor, by itself, is membership of the British Association for Counselling.

However, just because somebody is a qualified professional in these three ways does not mean automatically that he or she will be the right person for you, or that he or she will automatically be right for anybody else. The personal qualities of the therapist – which we shall look at shortly – are probably even more important. This, at least, is what quite a lot of the published research suggests, and it seems common sense too.

At the same time, there are still quite a lot of very good counsellors around who had no formal training because this did not exist when they started. However, they should still have a supervisor, belong to an organisation with some national standing and a published code of conduct, and they should be undertaking some kind of training for themselves by regularly attending conferences or seminars.

Psychotherapists

The best qualified counsellors are also qualified psychotherapists. This means that they will have successfully completed at least a five-year training course, followed by a period of at least a year working under the close supervision of a training psychotherapist. Of course, they may be completing this final year when you see them, and this almost certainly means you will get a very good service from them: they want to do well, they have all the help they need, and they are, incidentally, likely to charge relatively low fees.

All psychotherapists worth the name have themselves been in psychotherapy or analysis as clients. Again, unless you find your therapist from an organisation which has this policy clearly stated for all to see, it is not safe to make the assumption, and you should ask. However, do not be put off by learning that your therapist still sees a therapist – from time to time the good ones go back in as part of their continuing self-development. It's more likely to be a good sign than a bad one.

Analysts similarly have had to complete their own analysis before they can qualify. They belong to analytical societies, which are listed in the Useful Addresses on page 112.

Personal qualities

None of us really wants to go to an average therapist – we find it very difficult to imagine that a special relationship can be possible without a very special person to make it with. What are the personal qualities we seek in a therapist?

Patience

One of the qualities people often mention they want in a helper is patience. But there is patience and there is patience.

What we mean by patience is that the person is willing to give us time without ever wanting to hurry us along. He or she will listen and not interrupt even when we are confused and uncertain about what we are saying. It is a bit like tolerance – we want the person to be willing to suppress any need on his or her part to react angrily to even the most stupid things we do, not to condemn us or criticise us when we do things which ought to be condemned or criticised. A patient person puts up with us without complaining.

At one level these may seem to be admirable qualities in a helper. Yet are they? People only need patience when they become impatient. They are tolerant because inside they feel intolerant, and have the strength or persistence to deny that feeling, or the cleverness to disguise it so it does not show. Surely there are some things here which we do not want in a therapist. When somebody lacks patience and tolerance inside, and has to suppress these feelings, this says something about his or her attitude to other people – that there is no true acceptance of them, that an effort has to be made each time to convert an inner rejection into an outward show of acceptance.

Do we really want the person to be patient and tolerant of us? Obviously we would prefer the therapist to accept us for who we are, to allow us the space to make choices for ourselves. Yet we also want a therapist to be human, to be able to be angry and, when necessary, to express this feeling in a helpful way.

Of course, we may not accept ourselves as who we are. We may think of ourselves as somebody who needs to be dealt with sharply when we lose our way, or as somebody who does stupid things and needs to be told about this. We may see ourselves as lazy, boring, embarrassing – or as dangerous individuals who hurt, frighten, manipulate, injure other people. We may see ourselves this way now. But if so, and if we are seriously looking to change ourselves, these are amongst the very qualities we want to change. So a therapist who agrees fundamentally with this view we have of ourselves is unlikely to be one who could pilot us through these changes. We will want somebody who listens and gives us time, and who does not stop listening when we condemn ourselves, but not somebody who can condemn us the way we do it.

Kindness

Are we looking for somebody who is kind? In one sense we are, and in another sense we are not. There is kindness and there is kindness.

To be kind to people is to some extent the same as being patient and tolerant towards them. Yet it also has the added dimension of gentleness and compassion. It means being considerate to people when they are tired and hurt, and it also means being generous to them. Kind people are givers, not takers. They help you because that is the sort of people they are.

Once more, when we put this under the microscope we find something we may not want. *They help you because this is what they are like*, because they have an inner need, a compulsion of some sort to help others, particularly those who are worse off than themselves. The problem here is that kindness can be an expression of the kind person's own needs, that these are being met not necessarily because of your need, but certainly because of theirs. The signal to deliver such help is something which must run close to being patronising – the feeling that somebody else is worse off. Kindness is without doubt an admirable quality in the world, a virtue which it would be foolish to condemn. Maybe we need more of it. But in a therapist? The issue that is of most concern is surely that the therapist who is *kind* is also able to distinguish between his or her needs and private compulsions, and our needs as the client.

Without this added extra we cannot be certain that we shall be told hard truths when they might help us. These truths may be suppressed out of mistaken kindness. We want to be certain that when the bad news is withheld it is because there is sound professional judgement guiding the therapist, not his or her own unconscious desperation or sense of superiority.

Haya Oakley of the Philadelphia Association was one of the

people we asked about this. What she said seems to sum up many of these points and to add to them also in a very subtle way. Just before the interview she had been talking to a trainee about her work.

She has a patient who was complaining to her recently that he had very little money and wanted to cut his sessions down, and towards the end of the session he was attacking her. She didn't know how to handle this, and the only way she could cope was by saying – right, you can start from next week, just coming once a week instead of twice. Then she felt she had messed it up. The next session he comes in, and what does he tell her? That he told the cleaning lady that he couldn't afford to pay her, and the lady was so good, and she said she'd come for nothing for a while. He also said he had told his boss that he was in debt, and the boss said, 'If only I had the money I would pay all your debts.' And he told the therapist, this isn't such a terrible world as I thought. He went on to say that this kindness had upset him and brought him to tears.

Now when she told me about these words – 'upset me' – that's the sort of thing I immediately underline in my mind. I find myself asking straight away, why should kindness upset him? Which kindness was he referring to particularly? What is he really saying in these words?

The point is that all this happened after he had flustered the trainee and got her to agree to cut down on the sessions. The story about the cleaning lady and the boss *upsetting* him by being kind carries a message for the trainee. He's telling her something about her having upset him by simply and so easily falling into his trap. Really, she should not have let him get away with it so easily because he particularly needs therapy, and she should have been hearing this need, and being there in such a way that would have enabled him to negotiate.

The trainee didn't really hear him. She went on the defensive, feeling that he was lining her up with a whole queue of people who were after his money, when the fact is that she is only a trainee and therefore charges very little compared to what he would pay otherwise. There's really no question that he can afford it. As you heard, he has a job, and he also has a cleaning lady. But he feels robbed and deprived as a person, and that makes him feel he has to deprive himself and cut back, and the thing he says he wants to cut back on is the therapy – the place where he feels less deprived and robbed, but the thing he dare not deserve. She gets confused and defensive and gives in – he's upset and he comes and tells her that what appears as kindness upsets him.

Warmth?

What about warmth – the capacity to feel caring about other people, and to show this openly. We want our helpers to be people who are comfortable with us, who can support us, who will not be all formal and clinical and cold and unfeeling.

Warmth must also be used – like patience, compassion, tolerance, gentleness, kindness, and all the rest of the virtues – with professional skill, not because the therapist is meeting some inner need of his or her own instead of our needs, and not because this is the thing to do if you are a therapist. We are at greater risk than we would wish to be if warmth is given us as a prop that maintains a habit of being propped up.

Haya Oakley again:

Warmth can be a bit tricky. Some people think that psychotherapy is to do with being helpful and kind and supportive, and I don't think that. I think that people can find therapists helpful, and I think that people can find the fact that they are in therapy supportive. The word 'warmth' is often linked with this. You see, patients complain from time to time that I'm not being supportive, and I tell them they are quite right, because the notion of support involves the acknowledgement that the other person is a cripple. I think it's a question of enabling the other person to recognise that they *are* in their own right. I think it's true that therapists become a prop during therapy, but they are making a mistake if they set themselves up to become a prop or see their role as offering support.

It comes down to this in the end: that a good therapist is somebody who knows what he or she is doing, who will not react to us unthinkingly and unsafely, responding to his or her needs when it is our needs that should be foremost. Yet we also want more than this, for we none of us want people for our therapists who cannot be spontaneous. A good therapist is a human being like us, capable of feeling all the things you and I can feel. They would not be of this world if they could not be impatient, mean, ungenerous, cold, harsh at times. There may be times when they have to be not at all nice to us. But they need a continuous capacity for looking this over, for checking what they are doing, for listening to the things we are saying that we might not hear for ourselves.

Risk

The problem, of course, is that personal qualities like these cannot be guaranteed in any relationship right from the start, and all we can do is take the risk. If you have any doubts about the sort of person a therapist is on this score, right at the beginning, even if all the evidence shows that he or she has been trained, is supervised, belongs to the right organisations, and all the rest of it – do not proceed.

If such doubts are not there at the start, and only begin to occur to you during the course of therapy, however, talk them over with the therapist. It may be the effect of transference, rather than a lack of the right qualities on the part of the therapist.

In the end, once you have checked on your potential therapist's training, it may well come down to whether you feel instinctively that he or she is the right person for you.

12   Variety of therapy

The therapy movement contains more than a hundred different varieties of therapy. Our next objective is to describe the most important of them so you can make a more informed choice if you decide to try therapy yourself or suggest it to somebody else. The main reason for the variety is that almost from the beginning therapists have tended to fall out with one another over the scientific basis of therapy and the techniques which should be used.

The long-term effect of these disagreements has been to enrich therapy. For one thing, it has meant that many useful ideas have been tried out which would otherwise have never seen the light of day. Secondly, although there were bitter quarrels in the early years of the movement, some of these led eventually to an interesting and useful cross-fertilisation of ideas. Thirdly, all this diversity gives clients and therapists a much wider choice.

Obviously this is not the place to attempt a detailed survey. Indeed, we shall use as our starting point an idea put forward by Sidney Bloch, in his book *What is Psychotherapy?*. He suggested that there are three main schools of thought in the therapy movement, the ones we have already referred to, namely 'psycho-dynamic', 'humanistic-existentialist' and 'behavioural'. These labels are now widely accepted as useful and accurate. We shall explain what they mean, and say a little bit about how the differences might affect your choice.

Psychology

Therapy has grown out of psychology, the systematic study of human and animal behaviour. This sets it apart from psychiatry, which in modern times at least, started from anatomy and physiology – the study of the body and how it works. To begin to understand the main branches of therapy, therefore, it is helpful to consider some of the detailed subject areas which psychology covers. Three of them are particularly important from our present point of view.

As we might expect, part of psychology is concerned with people and personality – what a person is, how we grow up, and what accounts for the differences between individuals. Another part considers and investigates social behaviour – the way we relate to one another and communicate, the effect this has on what we are able to do, and the way we perceive the world, ourselves and other people. A third area which psychologists have investigated in great detail is behaviour itself – what is it, what causes it to happen, what will alter it?

Broadly speaking, psycho-dynamic therapy has grown out of the part of psychology concerned with personality and its development. This is the area where Freud made his greatest contribution to the science, and the early quarrels in the movement were often about whether he was right in his views as to the main influences.

The existential-humanistic therapies tend to be more concerned with people as social beings, and have largely grown from scientific work on how we communicate, perceive ourselves, and relate to one another.

Behavioural therapy is built upon studies of the way behaviour is modified according to the different events which happen around us – whether these are experienced as 'reinforcing' or 'inhibiting', that is to say, whether they are likely to make us want to do the same thing again, or not. This is the branch of therapy most closely connected with the theories of conditioning.

Psycho-dynamic approach

Psycho-dynamic therapy is essentially interested in investigating the connection between childhood experience and adult personality, and its main methods consist of free association, interpretation and the use of transference, all of which we described earlier. In this kind of therapy, therefore, you are likely to spend quite a lot of time rediscovering events from your early years which you had forgotten, exploring the feelings associated with these events, reliving many of these feelings, and gaining a new insight into the way you have been influenced by what happened.

The least diluted form of psycho-dynamic therapy is generally reckoned to be a Freudian or a Jungian analysis.

Both are likely to regard dreams as an important source of material for the analysis – Freud called the interpretation of dreams 'the royal road to a knowledge of the unconscious – the securest foundation of psycho-analysis'.

Psycho-dynamic ideas are also widely used by counsellors, but in a much more diluted form. For example, all counsellors are likely to encourage you to speak freely using the free association rule. Those trained in psycho-dynamics will try to help you gain insight into problems by drawing parallels between past and present. But they will not be so likely to use transference, and are probably less interested in detailed dream analysis.

Our research for this book suggests that the bulk of the medium-and long-term therapy – therapy which lasts more than one year and consists of at least one session per week – uses psycho-dynamic principles. At one end of the spectrum this will be very like analysis, except that the client is seen less often. At the other end, it can be very like psycho-dynamic counselling. The basic strategy is the same – to trace current distress back to its early origins with the therapist acting as guide.

So psycho-dynamic therapy can be like taking a lot of day-trips into childhood, looking round, drawing conclusions, and coming back to the present to apply what you have learned. At first this can be distressing, because the bits you visit are the most painful bits. As you go deeper into therapy the trips become longer, you learn more, and by the end – if the therapy is successful – you should feel not only comfortable but positively rewarded by revisiting even the worst parts. When the process is complete, you can go back into any part of the past for enrichment, by yourself and as often as you like.

Existential and humanistic therapy

Intuitive approach
But is this really necessary? Many therapists who work outside this tradition think not. They argue that there is an alternative strategy, which is to stay very much in the present, and to look forwards to what you wish to become next. This is summed up in the well-known axiom that 'today is the first day of the rest of your life'.

Many of us begin therapy by not being at all certain what we want out of life right now, and even less sure what kind of person we wish to become in future. So this strategy can help us clarify a great many important issues. If we are to decide what we want to be, we have to decide what we are right now. The strategy is a good way of getting us to look deeply at many aspects of our present-day life and relationships. Naturally, the effects of past experience play a large part in shaping us and our perceptions of ourselves, so we need to understand the past too. But it could be argued sensibly that there is no need to stir up painful memories unless they are actually stopping us from becoming what we want to be. Sleeping dogs need only be disturbed if they are in the way.

Person-Centred Therapy and Gestalt Therapy are good examples of this approach. The basic notion is that the client – as Brian Thorne put it earlier – 'knows what he or she wants'. That is to say, the client is assumed to have a basic intuitive knowledge of what he or she is like now, and wants to become in future. The therapist respects this, and therefore follows where the client leads, seeing the client's world the same way the client sees it, being with the client as a companion on the way, sharing the experience but accepting that a therapist cannot take over as the expert guide.

So this kind of therapy is about becoming a person – authentic, real, autonomous, and integrated, not false, unable to feel, and basically disintegrated. Interpretation under these circumstances is usually an expression of empathy; only on rare occasions will it be technical or analytical.

In psycho-dynamic therapy there is a strong tendency to regard self-knowledge as more dependent on reason than intuition. The therapist is assumed a lot of the time to know more about you than you know yourself, and expected to provide some leadership. In the person-centred approach the intuitive self-knowlege of the client is assumed to be there all the time, waiting, as it were, to be acknowledged and encouraged.

Rationalist approach

At the same time there are other existential or humanistic therapies which work in a less intuitive way, whilst still starting in the present and looking to the future. The therapist assumes the role of guide, applying his or her expertise to help the client gain a more rational self-understanding.

For example, in Personal Construct Therapy, the therapist may employ paper and pencil methods by getting the client to list the common factors and the differences between people who have influenced him or her, or who are associated with rewarding or difficult experiences in life. You may also be encouraged to do 'homework' between sessions to clarify the issues.

Fantasy drawings which help you discover how you see yourself and others may also be used. Within this, and similar ways of working, language is likely to be regarded the key to understanding your view of the world and how you arrived at it. The way we think and feel is closely bound up with who we are, and when we express this through speech, with all its limitations, we say more than we realise about who we are and the limitations we place on ourselves.

It is also obvious that when you work in this kind of way, whilst feelings are of supreme importance, you are also looking at yourself from a rational standpoint – applying the force of reason to your self-analysis. Some of the approaches in the existential and humanistic tradition go quite a long way down this road, seeing therapy as a rational re-training of the mind of the client. This may have disadvantages in the hands of therapists who are too rational and not empathetic enough, but then any therapy can suffer from this, and there are certainly many who benefit from a rational approach.

In this context we should mention Rational Emotive Therapy (RET) and Transactional Analysis (TA) as examples. They are dissimilar in many respects, but both set out to enable you to change yourself into what you want to be by identifying rationally why you make the sort of choices which are characteristic of you – especially those choices which may not be in your own best interests. Both these varieties of therapy are undergoing something of a resurgence at present, mainly because they have attracted some very talented and sensitive therapists.

Behaviour therapy

Behaviour therapies are closely connected with the so-called 'behavioural' school of thought in experimental psychology and their knowledge base consists of the scientific theories which account for what is called 'conditioning'. Most of us probably use this word fairly loosely – for example, we say we have been 'conditioned' to act in such and such a way by our parents, or by the kind of society we grew up in. In fact there are very precise experimental findings which show how an organism can be conditioned, or deconditioned.

The objective of behavioural therapies is to modify the behaviour of the client in a desired direction. This can be especially helpful to clients whose lives are distrupted by obsessive or phobic behaviour patterns – such as a total, twenty-four hour a day obsession with hand-washing, or a phobic reaction to flying which stops somebody taking a promotion which depends on international travel. We all probably tend to develop ritual behaviours when under stress – putting clothes away in a certain order, for example, or rearranging things on the table in front of us into straight lines. When this kind of thing begins to take over our lives it can become not only inconvenient and embarrassing, but also very distressing for ourselves and those close to us.

Behaviour therapy helps us by using a variety of techniques which alter the rewards we get from these behaviours. First, the ritual is carefully studied by the therapist, and analysed in terms of the sort of sights or sounds which trigger it. Care is taken to grade these, so that stimuli which would only produce a mild reaction can be distinguished from ones which trigger a major reaction. For example, imagining yourself sitting in an aeroplane waiting for take-off would lead to a mild attack of the fear of flying; actually being on board the plane would produce a massive anxiety attack.

Once the condition under which attacks occur have been analysed, the therapist works out a specific strategy for that client and the two discuss it and set up a contract. Then the treatment begins, usually with the therapist teaching the client how to relax. The eventual aim is for the client to be able to go into the threatening situation in a completely relaxed frame of mind so the anxiety does not occur and the ritual, or phobic reaction does not take place.

What happens next depends on the strategy adopted by the therapist. One approach – sometimes called 'laddering' – would be to take the client step by step through a range of experiences starting with those that trigger a mild reaction and working up to the severe ones. Each time the client is taught how to relax, and the next stage is not entered until relaxation is achieved. In time the client learns how to be relaxed with something that once terrified him or her.

Another approach is called 'flooding' – the client is placed in the frightening situation at its most severe, without any help being available, and, of course, survives it. For example, if fear of flying is the problem, the client is placed on the plane at take-off. If this sounds cruel, however, remember that it can only happen if it has already been agreed at the contract stage, after careful study by the therapist of the actual problem the client faces.

In a third kind of strategy, the therapist acts as a model,

proving to the client that the stimulus does not hurt – like a parent might get a child used to handling a tame mouse by doing it himself or herself, talking all the time in a relaxed way to the child. A mixture of all three methods might be used, but whatever the strategy it is based on thorough research, and a clear contract is agreed with the client each time.

This kind of therapy, of course, deals directly with what a psycho-dynamic therapist would regard as the symptoms, not the causes of the problem. However, research shows that it can achieve excellent results where there are clear symptoms capable of direct modification. It is also argued that the method is less important than the therapist – and this is probably true. After all, at each step of the way, whichever strategy is used, the relationship between therapist and client has to be one of trust. Otherwise it is unlikely that the client would persevere.

This brand of therapy began in the context of hospital medicine and academic psychology. It was largely pioneered by Hans Eysenck at the Institute of Psychiatry in London, and has been very influential in psychiatry generally. If you feel it can be of use to you, or somebody you know, the best way of pursuing the matter is to talk to your family practitioner about it in the first place, or follow up the appropriate information in the Useful Addresses listed on pages 109–13.

Other therapies

There are many varieties of therapy we have not mentioned. For example, we have said nothing about group therapy, and this can be just right for certain people, possibly most of all for those who are experiencing difficulty being open and honest in relating generally to colleagues, family, and age peers. Nor have we mentioned the therapies which combine body awareness with other forms of self-awareness. The best-known version, with a pedigree that can be traced back to Reich, one of Freud's early associates, is called bio-energetics. We have included more information about groups and body-work therapy in the list of Useful Addresses on pages 109–13.

Two kinds of therapy have been deliberately excluded, not in any sense because we disagree with them, but because they do not fit our self-imposed definition of the therapy movement. Hypnotherapy is one. Here we are uncertain as to the therapy training which practitioners receive. We recommend that you check this out individually. The other is co-counselling, in which clients are trained to work in pairs without a professional therapist present. This is not included because we concentrated on the professional therapies. Both these can easily be traced by you without our help if you wish to pursue them.

Making the choice

The wide variety of therapy is a reality. In practice, the wide choice it offers may be an illusion. First, despite the growth of the movement during the last few years, most of us live some distance away from the nearest therapist, he or she may be booked up, and many of the varieties of therapy have only a handful of qualified practitioners. This situation will certainly ease within a few years, but you may have to live with it for some time yet. Secondly, however, choice on the basis of what the therapist believes is probably not as important to the client as it is to the therapist. The most effective choice you can make is to choose a good therapist, and this means somebody who suits you personally, not necessarily somebody who happens to practise from a particular philosophy.

So a certain amount of shopping around is necessary. If you can do this in the first instance by talking to organisations and reading books rather than actually starting work with a therapist it is best to do so. Clients who start therapy, give it up, and start again with somebody else too many times may be suspected of lacking commitment and become disillusioned. Nevertheless, if you do decide that a therapist you work with is wrong for you, and the therapist accuses you angrily of lacking commitment or tries to make you feel bad about leaving, this is probably a sign that you are right to leave. Check back on what we said earlier about interpretation, and if what is happening does not fit the three criteria, tell your therapist so, and negotiate your way out.

Another consideration in all this is fees. There is a large body of opinion in the movement that fees are part of the safety that therapy offers. First, if you do not pay, it is harder to sack the therapist should things go wrong. Secondly, paying means that you have bought the time, and you are not being given it out of charity, or some mistaken idea of kindness. Thirdly, it means you are investing in yourself, and this is something therapy encourages in a wider sense. The opponents of this view say that people pay in any case in other ways – investing time, energy, and trouble in therapy. Money, they argue, makes very little difference.

In 1988 fees range from £10 per fifty-minute session upwards, usually depending on what the client says he or she can pay. There are very few people who charge more than £25 per fifty-minute session, but they exist, and there is no reason to suppose they do any better job than the rest. Counselling is more often free than psychotherapy or analysis, but this is usually intended for desperate people facing an emergency and financially dependent on partners who have let them down. Whatever the arrangement – some counselling centres do not charge fees but ask for a donation – the question of fees is universally open to negotiation.

13 Possible futures

Voluntary helplessness

The diversity of the therapy movement should not make us
forget the common factors. All therapy – however it is
practised – is the same kind of thing, built around the same
basic activities. First, therapy provides a confiding and
confidential relationship where we can be helped. The details
of what the therapist believes and the methods he or she uses
are always secondary to this. We can tell our troubles as they
really are for the first time and be safely heard.

There is an awesome risk in this. At the moment of
disclosure we cease to protect ourselves, and we do this with
the sole purpose that somebody else shall meet us in our most
vulnerable state. We become voluntarily helpless. No
particular brand of therapy can be devised which will take
away this risk. And we can only take the risk when we have
learned to trust the therapist to know our deepest pain, and not
to add to the hurt. All therapies, however else they may differ,
depend equally on trust.

Relief

The act of telling brings its own reward. Until we tell we do not
realise how much our troubles cost us. They have first call
upon all our resources. They sap our ability to be content with
what we are, forcing us to work harder at being something we
are not, and making us hide the part of ourselves we feel we
cannot share. They tire us and leave us isolated. When we talk
about them with somebody whom we can trust we put down at
least part of the heavy burden and that in itself brings us a
measure of relief. In the words of the old proverb, a trouble
shared is a trouble halved.

At the same time, because what we say will be confidential
to that relationship, we have the choice of taking no other
action but this. Nobody else need know. We can simply say how
we feel, feel a bit better as a result, and do nothing more. If this
is what we decide to do we hurt nobody and disappoint nobody.
We are free to feel better and to leave things there, using in
any way we choose the measure of comfort we have gained. The
rewards of telling, the need for confidentiality, the freedom to
choose when to stop – none of these depends on any particular
doctrine.

Empowering

Yet if we wish to stay and try to get more than this we can do
so. All forms of therapy offer us not only the relief of safe self-
disclosure, but also an opportunity to look more deeply at what
we have said, at what we feel which we cannot put into words.
They empower us to examine the past, the present, and the
future from that starting point. They make available to us the
energy to attend to ourselves, the space to explore our feelings,
the time to discover what we really want to do, or to have, or to
be.

This is because whatever therapy we might choose, it will be
based on some explanation of how we came to feel our pain. It
will have a way of helping us to see that even though the
events which caused the pain are for ever part of who we are,
we need not be permanently hurt by them, and may even gain
from them. Therapy does not make us feel better in spite of our
pain, but shows us how to grow because of it. The explanations
differ from therapist to therapist, from school of thought to
school of thought. Yet all the explanations have this single
purpose.

Shared insight

Furthermore, these explanations are always shared. In the
course of therapy, the therapist may find things out about you
which you never knew yourself, but none of this can be used
until it becomes your own truth, which you believe in your own
way. Therapy depends upon mutuality. It is not a one-sided
affair in which you are mysteriously operated upon by a
benevolent agent and magically get better. It is more like
education than surgery. The therapist and the client learn
together or there is no therapy.

They learn within the theories of the therapist, of course.

Inevitably all therapy helps its clients make sense of their situation by using the philosophy and values of the theory in which the therapist is trained and to which he or she is committed. It occurs subtly and naturally, not as a series of brain-taxing lessons in the concepts of theoretical psychology, but by the steady osmosis of shared perceptions and belief. It is not drummed in – it rubs off.

What really matters is that the therapy is based on a view of people which accords them total respect for their uniqueness. The ideas which are used during the meetings are less important than the fact that such meetings take place.

Reward

All useful therapy has one more feature in common: it has to justify the hope of the client that he or she can gain from it. Again there are many different ways of describing this hope and its attainment. For example, we could say that the client may end his or her therapy feeling more complete as a person; able to live life to the full more often; being less crippled by pain from the past; or with more freedom from distressing behaviour patterns. How the thing is described by therapists is often a matter of doctrine and couched in therapists' jargon.

But again what you call it is less significant than the experience itself. You go into therapy as one kind of person with a certain kind of life, and you come out of it maybe as a different kind of person or the same kind, but with the possibility in your own hands of creating a different kind of life. Therapy, at the bottom line, gives you options. In a world which demands change from all of us, therapy equips us to decide whether to change or not, when to change, and how to change if we wish to. It does not force us to change. It makes it easier if we want to.

The reward of therapy, then, is not the fact of change. We can go through the process successfully and decide not to do anything about our concerns. The reward is that we have the option now to do something if we so wish, whereas before therapy we did not have this option. Furthermore, this is not a prize we collect only at the end of weeks or months or years of therapy. If the therapy is working we are constantly aware of its rewards even though we may go through long periods when we seem to be getting nowhere. Nothing in good therapy is hopeless.

Not perfect

And bad therapy? We have no wish to deny that it happens –
indeed, we have spelled out many of the ways in which it
occurs, and suggested what you can do to avoid them, or, if this
fails, what you can do about it. Any profession is bound to have
its share of people who are not up to the mark.

Nevertheless, the signs are that therapy is much more likely
to be improving than becoming worse. Training, as we have
seen, is generally longer these days, and more rigorous. The
people going into the profession are a wider cross-section of
society, too, because more training facilities are available. If
there is a problem currently it is that there are not enough
therapists in the right places, and no clear career structure
available to them which might help to rationalise the
distribution.

But in any case, the therapy movement as a whole consists of
people who do not set out to be perfect, just as they do not
demand perfection from their clients. For both client and
therapist the goal is to be good enough, and to see where that
leads.

Influencing society

It could lead in several directions. As the movement grows it is
likely to have a wider influence on society in general, helping
to change attitudes, subtly adding to our experience of good
communication, persuading us to know ourselves better, to
take less for granted in the way we treat one another. It is a
fitting product of our times, suited to an ever more crowded
world where we travel more widely than any of our ancestors
did, take less for granted, ask more questions, live longer, and
meet more strangers.

So what are its possible futures? Maybe it will reduce the
number of permanent victims – the victims of child cruelty, of
war and tragedy, of bereavement, oppression and exploitation.
The movement certainly offers this hope to those who seek its
help. Maybe it will enable many of the members of one
generation to put an end to the cycle of deprivation, whereby
the hurts of the child get passed on to that child's children in
perpetuity. Maybe it will alter significantly our patterns of
child care, or the quality of our family life.

Maybe it will do none of these things, but become ossified in
some institutionalised bureaucracy, or fall apart through
dissension and lack of leadership. Or maybe it will challenge

too boldly the power of those who hurt and exploit others, so they subtly curtail its growth by ensuring that it is reserved only for people who have 'real problems', and not for 'real people' with ordinary problems. There are some who would argue that this is happening already. Whatever future emerges for the movement, it will be worth watching.

In the meantime, what about you?

Yourself

We said at the beginning that we wanted to make it easier for you to answer for yourself the question: is this the kind of help that I need or could make use of, or which would be useful to somebody else I know personally?

The only safe part of this question, of course, is the first part, the bit about yourself. Therapy is a very personal business, not something we can really decide on behalf of others. They can be encouraged to consider it, but ultimately they can only answer for themselves.

So what about you? Where would you like to start?

Like us, you can only begin with questions. They are the sort of questions which might have been put to you in that warm room up the stairs in the counselling centre, or the sort of questions the radio counsellor might have put to Sue, aged 26, who was having problems with her boyfriend. They are the universal questions of therapy.

What are you doing with your life that you do not wish to do? How did you become the person you are, instead of the person you would like to be? Which bit of you that hurts has not been heard? When will you decide to stop coping and accept that there is something better?

In therapy these questions can be put a million ways, answered a million ways, but heard only one way that matters – with unconditional acceptance of you and your intrinsic value as a person in your own right. Or, as you might say, with love.

In the studio

Back in the basement studio, the counsellor is still listening to his first caller. We have missed a lot of what was said, because we were busy with other things. But we are not too late to find out how things turned out.

'Sue,' says the counsellor, 'thank you for telling me all that. It can't have been easy for you. It sounds as though you are very lonely and very hurt and very angry.' 'I am,' says Sue, accepting this at last, weeping now. 'Tell me, when did you first feel this way?'

'I suppose,' she says, 'I've been lonely all my life. I'm only just beginning to realise how lonely. And angry. But I don't want to come to terms with it any more, I want to do something about it. I've had enough of sitting around and waiting and trying to get people to fit me into their lives, and coping and being used.'

'Yes,' says the counsellor.

'I think I have the right to be angry.'

'You have that right,' says the counsellor.

'All my life I've been fobbed off with second best this and second best that and expected to put up with it and not complain. Now I've had enough. I shall have to tell him.'

'Yes,' says the counsellor.

'How can anybody treat somebody they love – or say they love – like this? How can they?'

'Mmm,' says the counsellor.

'Well I'm not going to let him.'

'Right.'

'I'll tell him. I'm frightened, but I shall tell him. I'll do it tonight, when he comes round to see me. I shall just have to say something.' She pauses and breathes deeply.

'Well, that's it I suppose. Thank you for your help. Thank you for listening to me,' says Sue. 'That's what we're here for,' says the counsellor.

Useful addresses

There is some counselling and therapy available on the NHS, so it's worth enquiring from your GP or your local branch of MIND. Contact their national headquarters for your nearest branch:

MIND (National Association for Mental Health)
22 Harley Street, London W1N 2ED. Tel: 01-637 0741

There are also a growing number of groups and organisations offering various forms of therapy to fee-paying clients. Some of these organisations offer reduced fees to people on low incomes, or work on a donation basis; others take a few referrals from the NHS. This is worth asking about if you contact them.

Counselling

British Association for Counselling
37a Sheep Street, Rugby, Warwickshire, CV21 3BX. Tel: 0788-78328/9
Provides information about counselling in your area.

Relate Marriage Guidance
Herbert Gray College, Little Church Street, Rugby, Warwickshire. Tel: 0788-73241
Provides information about marriage guidance counselling in your area.

Westminster Pastoral Foundation
23 Kensington Square, London W8 5HN. Tel: 01-937 6956
One of the foremost training organisations for counsellors and therapists, WPF also offers individual, couple and group counselling. WPF can refer you to an affiliated counselling centre in your area.

Alton Counselling Service
Friends Meeting House, Church Street, Alton, Hampshire. Tel: 0420-83459
Offers short-term humanistic and psychoanalytic counselling.

Birmingham Women's Counselling and Therapy Centre
43 Ladywood Middleway, Birmingham, B16 8HA
Offers individual counselling and therapy from a feminist perspective.

Blackpool and Fylde Counselling Centre
Beaufort Avenue, Bispham, Blackpool. Tel: 0253-56624/866976
Offers individual counselling.

Carrs Lane Counselling Centre
Carrs Lane Church, Birmingham, B4 7SX. Tel: 021-643 6363
Offers counselling to individuals and couples.

Isis Centre
43 Little Clarendon Street, Oxford, OX1 2HU. Tel: 0865-56648
Offers individual, marital, family and group counselling along psychoanalytic principles. Also offers information about other counselling resources in the area.

Women's Counselling and Therapy Service
Oxford Chambers, Oxford Place, Leeds, LS1 3AX. Tel: 0532-455725
Offers counselling and psychoanalytic therapy from a feminist perspective; also runs workshops and provides a 'drop-in' service.

Norwich Centre for Personal and Professional Development
7 Earlham Road, Norwich, NR2 3RA. Tel: 0603-617709
Offers person-centred counselling for individuals and couples; also organises workshops and lectures.

Tom Allan Centre
23 Elmbank Street, Glasgow, G64 1TP. Tel: 041-221 1535
Offers counselling for individuals, families and groups.

Therapy

British Association of Psychotherapists
Secretary: Mrs Judith Lawrence, 121 Hendon Lane, London N3 3PR. Tel: 01-346 1747
One of the foremost training organisations; offers individual psychoanalytic psychotherapy.

Arbours Association
41a Weston Park, London N8 9SY. Tel: 01-340 7646
Offers individual existential psychotherapy; also runs a short-stay crisis centre and long-stay households for people in stress.

Association for Group and Individual Psychotherapy
29 St Mark's Crescent, London NW1 7TU. Tel: 01-485 9141
Offers individual psychoanalytic psychotherapy.

Association of Humanistic Psychology Practitioners
General Secretary: Judith Dell, 45 Litchfield Way, London
NW11 6NU. Referrals: 01-928 7102
A coordinating organisation for the human potential/growth
movement. AHPP offers information and a list of humanistic
therapists in your area.
Camden Psychotherapy Unit
25–31 Tavistock Place, London WC1H 9SE. Tel: 01-388 2071
ext 28
Offers psychoanalytic psychotherapy to Camden residents.
Centre for Personal Construct Psychology
132 Warwick Way, London SW1V 4JD. Tel: 01-834 8875
Offers individual personal construct therapy.
Clinic of Psychotherapy
Garden Flat, 26 Belsize Square, London NW3 4HU. Tel:
01-903 6455 (answering service)
Offers individual psychoanalytic psychotherapy.
Ealing Psychotherapy Centre
St Martin's Rooms, Hale Gardens, London W3. Tel: 01-993
5185
Offers psychoanalytic psychotherapy.
Gestalt Centre
Administrator: Judith Leary-Tanner, 64 Warwick Road,
St Albans, Hertfordshire, AL1 4DL. Tel: 0727-64806
The centre offers individual therapy and runs a variety of
workshops and groups.
Institute of Psychotherapy and Social Studies
5 Lake House, South Hill Park, London NW3 2SH. Tel: 01-794
4147
Offers humanistic and psychoanalytic therapy to individuals,
families and groups.
Institute of Transactional Analysis
BM Box 4104, London WC1 3XX.
Offers individual and group transactional analysis, can put
you in touch with practitioners in your area.
Lincoln Clinic and Institute for Psychotherapy
77 Westminster Bridge Road, London, SE1 7HS. Tel: 01-928
7211/01-261 9236
Offers psychoanalytic psychotherapy.
London Centre for Psychotherapy
19 Fitzjohn's Avenue, London NW3 5JY. Tel: 01-435 0873
Offers psychoanalytic psychotherapy.
Manchester Feminists Therapists Group
27 Victoria Park Road, Whalley Range, Manchester 16.
Offers therapy from a feminist perspective.

Morpeth Centre for Psychotherapy
4 Market Place West, Morpeth, Northumberland, NE16 1HE.
Tel: 0670-57434
Offers individual and group humanistic therapy and counselling;
also runs workshops and groups.

Nafsiyat – The Inter-Cultural Therapy Centre
278 Seven Sisters Road, London, N4 2HY. Tel: 01-263 4130
Offers psychoanalytic psychotherapy taking special account of
cultural factors.

North London Personal Consultation Practice
17A Templars Crescent, London N3 3QR. Tel: 01-349 9399
Offers individual and group psychoanalytic psychotherapy.

North London Centre for Group Therapy
138 Bramley Road, Oakwood, London N14 4HU. Tel: 01-440
1451
Offers individual, couple, family and group psychotherapy.

Philadelphia Association
14 Peto Place, London NW1 4DT. Tel: 01-486 9012
Offers existential psychotherapy.

South London Psychotherapy Group
19 Broom Water, Teddington, Middlesex, TW11 9QT.
Offers psychoanalytic psychotherapy.

Spectrum
49 Croftdown Road, London NW5 1EL. Tel: 01-485 5259
Offers individual therapy, counselling and workshops, all from a
humanistic perspective.

Tavistock Clinic
120 Belsize Lane, London NW3 5BA. Tel: 01-435 7111
Offers psychoanalytic psychotherapy *only* within its North
London catchment area. Also one of the foremost training bodies
for psychotherapists.

Women's Therapy Centre
6 Manor Gardens, London N7 6LA. Tel: 01-263 6200
Offers long- and short-term psychoanalytic and humanistic
psychotherapy; also group therapy and workshops – all from a
feminist perspective.

Psycho-analysis

British Psycho-Analytic Society
63 New Cavendish Street, London W1M 7RD. Tel: 01-580 4952/3
Members of the Society offer analysis with a Freudian/Kleinian
orientation. The society also runs the London Clinic of
Psycho-Analysis (at the same address) which offers low-cost
analysis by its trainees.

Society of Analytic Psychology
1 Daleham Gardens, London NW3 5BY. Tel: 01-435 7696
Members offer Jungian analysis. The society also runs the C.G.
Jung Clinic (at the same address) which offers low-cost
analysis by trainees.
Association of Jungian Analysts
Flat 3, 7 Eton Avenue, London NW3 5EL. Tel: 01-794 8711
Members offer Jungian analysis.
Group-Analytic Practice
88 Montagu Mansions, London W1H 1LF. Tel: 01-935
3103/3085
Offers group psycho-analysis.

Further reading

A vast number of books have been written about the various forms of therapy, but the ones we've listed here are good starting-points for further reading. Most of these books are available in paperback. If you have difficulty finding them in your local bookshop or library, two London bookshops will supply by mail:

Karnac Books
58 Gloucester Road, London SW7 4QY
Compendium
234 Camden High Street, London NW1 8QS

Guides to therapy

Sidney Bloch, *What is Psychotherapy?*, OUP, 1982.
Sidney Bloch, *An Introduction to the Psychotherapies*, OUP, 1985.
Windy Dryden (ed), *Individual Therapy in Britain*, Harper and Row, 1984.
Joel Kovel, *A Complete Guide to Therapy*, Penguin, 1982.
Lindsay Knight, *Talking to a Stranger: A Consumer's Guide To Therapy*, Fontana, 1986.
John Rowan and Windy Dryden (eds), *Innovative Therapy in Britain*, OUP, 1988.

Personal accounts of counselling, therapy and analysis

Marie Cardinal, *The Words To Say It*, Picador, 1984.
Rosemary Dinnage, *One to One: Experiences of Psychotherapy*, Viking, 1988.
Sarah Ferguson, *A Guard Within*, Flamingo, 1987.
Anne France, *Consuming Psychotherapy*, Free Association Books, 1988.
Ronald Fraser, *In Search of a Past*, Verso, 1984.

Peter Fuller, *Marches Past*, Chatto and Windus, 1986.
Nini Herman, *My Kleinian Home*, Quartet, 1985.
Marion Milner, *The Hands of the Living God: An Account of a Psychoanalytic Treatment*, Virago, 1988.
Susan Oldfield, *The Counselling Relationship*, Routledge and Kegan Paul, 1983.
Robyn Skinner and John Cleese, *Families and How to Survive Them*, Methuen, 1983.
Stuart Sutherland, *Breakdown*, Weidenfeld and Nicolson, 1976.

Psychoanalytic therapies

The two founding fathers of psycho-analysis, Sigmund Freud and C.G. Jung, wrote extensively about their theories. Freud is easy to read and much of his work is published in paperback by Penguin. Jung is harder going, but try *Dreams* and *Man and his Symbols*. Jung's writings are published in Ark Paperbacks by Routledge, and a good introduction is Freida Fordham's *An Introduction to Jung's Psychology*, Penguin, 1966.
Virginia Axline, *Dibs: In Search of Self*, Penguin, 1971.
Bruno Bettelheim, *Freud and Man's Soul*, Chatto and Windus/The Hogarth Press, 1983.
Bruno Bettelheim, *A Good Enough Parent*, Thames and Hudson, 1987.
John Bowlby, *Child Care and the Growth of Love*, Penguin, 1965.
Patrick Casement, *On Learning From the Patient*, Tavistock, 1985.
Erik H. Erikson, *Childhood and Society*, Paladin, 1977.
Sheila Ernst and L. Goodison, *In Our Own Hands*, Women's Press, 1981.
Sheila Ernst and Marie Maguire, *Living with the Sphinx: Papers from the Women's Therapy Centre*, Women's Press, 1987.
Michael Fordham, *Jungian Psychotherapy*, Wiley, 1978.
Nini Herman, *Why Psychotherapy?*, Free Association Books, 1987.
Robert Hobson, *Forms of Feeling: The Heart of Psychotherapy*, Tavistock, 1985.
Melanie Klein, *Envy and Gratitude*, Virago, 1988.
Alice Miller, *The Drama of Being a Child*, Virago, 1987.
Alice Miller, *For Your Own Good*, Virago, 1987.
Alice Miller, *Thou Shalt Not Be Aware*, Pluto, 1986.
Juliet Mitchell (ed), *The Melanie Klein Reader*, Penguin, 1986.

Juliet Mitchell, *Psychoanalysis and Feminism*, Penguin, 1975.
Charles Rycroft, *Psychoanalysis and Beyond*, Chatto and Windus/The Hogarth Press, 1985.
David Stafford-Clark, *What Freud Really Said*, Penguin, 1967.
Anthony Storr, *The Art of Psychotherapy*, Secker and Warburg/Heinemann, 1979.
Neville Symington, *The Analytic Experience: Lectures from the Tavistock*, Free Association Books, 1986.
D.W. Winnicott, *The Child, the Family and the Outside World*, Penguin, 1985.
D.W. Winnicott, *The Family and Individual Development*, Social Science Paperbacks, 1968.
D.W. Winnicott, *Home is Where We Start From*, Penguin, 1986.

Existential and humanistic therapies

Joseph Berke and Mary Barnes, *Two Accounts of a Journey Through Madness*, Penguin, 1972.
Eric Berne, *Games People Play*, Penguin, 1968.
Eric Berne, *Sex in Human Loving*, Penguin, 1973.
Eric Berne, *What Do You Say After You Say Hello?*, Corgi, 1975.
Joel Fagan and Irma Lee Shepherd, *Gestalt Therapy Now*, Penguin, 1972.
Thomas Harris, *I'm Ok – You're Ok*, Pan, 1973.
R.D. Laing, *The Politics of Experience*, Penguin, 1970.
R.D. Laing, *The Politics of the Family*, Penguin, 1971.
R.D. Laing, *The Divided Self*, Penguin, 1974.
R.D. Laing and Aaron Esterson, *Sanity, Madness and the Family*, Penguin, 1970.
Peter Lomas, *The Case for a Personal Psychotherapy*, OUP, 1981.
Peter Lomas, *The Limits to Interpretation*, Penguin, 1987.
Alexander Lowen, *The Language of the Body*, Collier (New York), 1969.
Alexander Lowen, *The Betrayal of the Body*, Collier (New York), 1969.
Alexander Lowen, *Bioenergetics*, Penguin, 1975.
Carl Rogers, *On Becoming a Person*, Constable, 1961.
Carl Rogers, *Encounter Groups*, Penguin, 1973.
Dorothy Rowe, *Choosing Not Losing*, Fontana, 1988.
Frederick Perls, *Gesalt Therapy Verbatim*, Bantam, 1972.
Frederick Perls, Ralph Hefferline and Paul Goodman, *Gestalt Therapy*, Souvenir Press, 1972.

Behavioural and directive therapies

Unfortunately, most of the literature on behavioural therapy is written for practitioners rather than clients, but *The Decline and Fall of the Freudian Empire* by Hans Eysenck (1986) and *Beyond Freedom and Dignity* by B.F. Skinner (1973), both published by Penguin, are readable books written by leading exponents of behavioural techniques.

Windy Dryden and William Golding (eds), *Cognitive-Behavioural Approaches to Psychotherapy*, Harper and Row, 1986 is an excellent introduction to a variety of therapies.

Index